HOTSPOTS
JERSEY

CW00375451

Written by Lindsay Hunt, updated by Carole French
Front cover photography courtesy of Alamy Images

Original design concept by Studio 183 Limited
Series design by the Bridgewater Book Company
Cover design/artwork by Lee Biggadike, Studio 183 Limited

Produced by the Bridgewater Book Company
The Old Candlemakers, West Street, Lewes, East Sussex BN7 2NZ, United Kingdom
www.bridgewaterbooks.co.uk
Project Editor: Emily Casey Bailey
Project Designer: Lisa McCormick

Published by Thomas Cook Publishing
A division of Thomas Cook Tour Operations Limited
PO Box 227, Units 15-16, Coningsby Road, Peterborough PE3 8SB, United Kingdom
email: books@thomascook.com
www.thomascookpublishing.com
+ 44 (0) 1733 416477

ISBN-13: 978-1-84157-566-7
ISBN-10: 1-84157-566-6

First edition © 2006 Thomas Cook Publishing
Text © 2006 Thomas Cook Publishing
Maps © 2006 Thomas Cook Publishing
Head of Thomas Cook Publishing: Chris Young
Project Editor: Diane Ashmore
Production/DTP Editor: Steven Collins

Printed and bound in Spain by Graficas Cems, Navarra, Spain

All rights reserved. No part of this publication may be reproduced, stored in a retrieval system or transmitted, in any form or by any means, electronic, mechanical, recording or otherwise, in any part of the world, without prior permission of the publisher. Requests for permission should be made to the publisher at the above address.

Although every care has been taken in compiling this publication, and the contents are believed to be correct at the time of printing, Thomas Cook Tour Operations Limited cannot accept any responsibility for errors or omission, however caused, or for changes in details given in the guidebook, or for the consequences of any reliance on the information provided. Descriptions and assessments are based on the author's views and experiences when writing and do not necessarily represent those of Thomas Cook Tour Operations Limited.

CONTENTS

SYMBOLS KEY

The following is a key to the symbols used throughout this book:

i	information office	✚	hospital	🍴	restaurant
🚍	bus stop	✈	airport	◻	café
✉	post office	↘	tip	🍸	bar
✝	church	🛍	shopping	◉	fine dining

T telephone   **F** fax   **e** email   **W** website address

a address   **L** opening times   **!** important

£ budget price   **££** mid-range price   **£££** most expensive

★ specialist interest   ★★ see if passing   ★★★ top attraction

---

INTRODUCTION
Getting to know Jersey

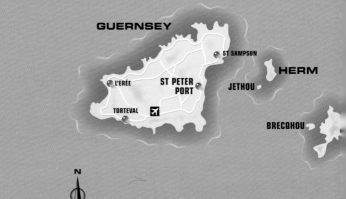

GUERNSEY

ST SAMPSON

HERM

L'ERÉE

ST PETER PORT

JETHOU

TORTEVAL

BRECQHOU

N

0   10 km

0   6 miles

UNITED KINGDOM

ENGLISH CHANNEL

CHANNEL
ISLANDS   ALDERNEY

GUERNSEY   HERM
          SARK

JERSEY

FRANCE

BURHOU

ST ANNE

ALDERNEY

THE ENGLISH CHANNEL

JERSEY

St Ouen

St John &
St Mary

ROZEL

St Peter

St Lawrence

St Martin
& Trinity

St Brelade

St Saviour

ULENTE

St Helier

St Clement
& Grouville

GOREY

ST HELIER

LA ROCQUE

Getting to know Jersey

Feeling soft sand between your toes and hearing waves lapping gently against the rocks, it is hard to imagine that somewhere there is a fast lane. On an island where the most strenuous pursuit is sipping coffee in one of the Continental-style cafés in St Helier, and where cars themselves seem to amble through the lanes, it doesn't get more peaceful than Jersey – rush hour aside!

Jersey lies in the Bay of Mont St Michel and is the largest of the Channel Islands. Drop a mental plumb-line due south of Weymouth, in Dorset, and you will find these chips of granite adrift somewhere west of Cherbourg – it is much closer to France than to the UK, and a good deal warmer and sunnier.

On a European scale, Jersey seems minute, but size isn't everything. In fact, the small scale of this seductive island is all part of its charm factor. Jersey is only around 15 km (9 miles) at its widest point and 8 km (5 miles) across, but every inch of its surface basks in southerly sunshine for the best part of the year.

Most visitors to the island arrive by plane or by fast ferry from Poole, Portsmouth and Weymouth in England or from St Malo in France. One of the first things they notice is the idyllic quaintness of the waterfront buildings, the green of the gentle hills beyond, the sheer size of the beaches and its rugged coastline.

Jersey experiences tides of up to 12 m (40 ft) every day, making it one of only a few places in the world with such extreme tidal conditions. The result is that its coastline changes constantly. For the energetic it is possible to walk over 3 km (2 miles) out seawards from the high water mark on an extreme tide!

● *The famous Jersey cows, prized for their creamy milk*

THE PARISHES

Jersey has 12 parishes, the UK equivalent of counties, each enjoying their own little bit of the dramatic coastline. The main resort and the 'city' of Jersey is St Helier on the south coast. However, St Brelade's Bay boasts of being the most southerly seaside town in the British Isles – a claim which is only occasionally challenged by St Helier. Some of the best beaches can be found along the south and eastern coast areas of St Clement and Grouville, although St Ouen, St Peter and St Brelade to the west also have their share. Along the north coast there are some beautiful little coves to explore: head for the parishes of St Martin, Trinity, St John and St Mary and look out for the signs to places such as Rozel Bay, Bonne Nuit Bay and Grève de Lecq. Two of the parishes, St Lawrence and St Saviour, are typified by their great expanses of open countryside where some of Jersey's prettiest wild flowers can be seen.

◐ *Jersey is the perfect seaside escape*

1066 AND ALL THAT...

The French call the Channel Islands 'Les Iles Anglo-Normandes'. They once formed part of the Duchy of Normandy, and passed into English hands with William the Conqueror. When King John lost control of his Norman possessions in 1204, the Channel Islanders were given the choice of reverting to France or remaining English. Shrewdly, they opted for the English side, on condition that they retained their own government and their ancient feudal privileges, relics of which they still hold today.

Thus the Channel Islands are within the British Isles, but they are not part of the United Kingdom. They have their own government and culture, their own laws and customs – even their own currency, postal services and tax systems. They bear allegiance to the Crown, but not to Westminster. Nor do they bear allegiance to Brussels – the Channel Islands are not full members of the EU. For the Channel Islanders, the British monarch is still the Duke of Normandy, and when they drink a loyal toast, they raise their glasses to 'The Queen, Our Duke'.

It is important to note that age-old rivalries still exist between the islanders, especially Jersey and Guernsey, who took separate sides in the English Civil War (1642).

SEIGNEURS & DAMES

The feudal system imposed by the Normans, in which parcels of land were granted by the king in exchange for military service, has long since lapsed on the larger islands. But some of the ancient manor houses remain, a few of which are still inhabited by descendants of the original seigneurial families. St Ouen's Manor (see map on page 12) is one.

North-east of Jersey, its nearest island neighbour, Sark, tantalizes political historians as the last remaining feudal society in Europe, still with its Seigneur or Dame as ruler, in name if not in practice. By one of those odd paradoxes so typical of the Channel Islands, however, it was never actually feudal during feudal times. Its seigneurial system dates only from 1565.

THE ENGLISH CHANNEL

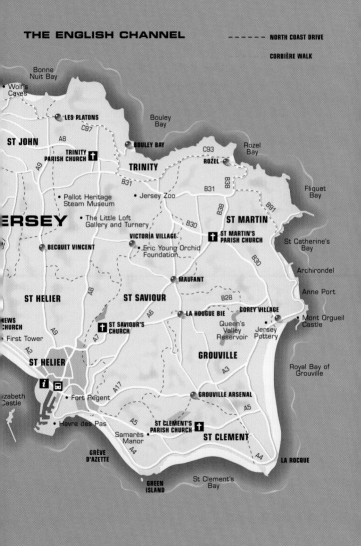

THE ENGLISH CHANNEL

- - - - - - NORTH COAST DRIVE

CORBIÈRE WALK

Bonne
Nuit Bay

• Wolf's
Caves

• LES PLATONS

C97

ST JOHN

A8

Bouley
Bay

• BOULEY BAY

TRINITY
PARISH CHURCH

A9

TRINITY

C93

Rozel
Bay

• ROZEL

B31

B38

Fliquet
Bay

ERSEY

B31

• Jersey Zoo

• Pallot Heritage
Steam Museum

• The Little Loft
Gallery and Turnery

B30

B8B

ST MARTIN

B91

• BECQUET VINCENT

VICTORIA VILLAGE

• Eric Young Orchid
Foundation

ST MARTIN'S
PARISH CHURCH

St Catherine's
Bay

B30

Archirondel

• MAUFANT

Anne Port

ST HELIER

A8

ST SAVIOUR

B28

A6

GOREY VILLAGE

Mont Orgueil
Castle

EWS
HURCH

A9

ST SAVIOUR'S
CHURCH

• LA HOUGUE BIE

Queen's
Valley
Reservoir

Jersey
Pottery

A7

• First Tower

GROUVILLE

A2

ST HELIER

A3

Royal Bay of
Grouville

izabeth
Castle

A17

i

• Fort Regent

GROUVILLE ARSENAL

A5

• Havre des Pas

A5

ST CLEMENT'S
PARISH CHURCH

Samarès
Manor

ST CLEMENT

A4

GRÈVE
D'AZETTE

A4

LA ROCQUE

GREEN
ISLAND

St Clement's
Bay

ROYAL MISTRESS

Lillie Langtry was the talk of the islands in the late 19th century. Born in St Saviour's parish in 1853, daughter of the Dean of Jersey, she became a celebrated society beauty. She was also an exceptionally vivacious and intelligent woman who founded her own acting company and toured around in her own train. This in itself was scandalous enough at the time, but Lillie achieved particular notoriety as an acknowledged mistress of the Prince of Wales, later Edward VII.

You can find out more about Lillie in the Jersey Museum, where you can see her ornate travelling case and a gorgeous portrait, *The Jersey Lily*, by Sir John Millais. Lillie was christened, married (twice) and buried in St Saviour's church. Her marble monument is signposted in the churchyard.

WORLD WAR II

World War II is an unforgettable period in Jersey's history as it, along with its neighbouring islands, was the only part of the British Isles to be invaded by the Germans. The Occupation Story is told in many museums all over the islands, and visitors often find them fascinating. Don't forget to look at the liberation monuments, too. You'll find Jersey's exuberant bronze sculpture of flag-waving revellers in Liberation Square. The best places to find out more are:

- **Occupation Tapestry** This impressive work tells the story of the island of Jersey during World War II and is the island's largest ever community project.
- **German Underground Hospital** This dark complex of tunnels, is one of the most chilling reminders of the German Occupation period on any of the Channel Islands.

BEATING THE TAXMAN

Low taxation makes Jersey and its neighbouring islands extremely attractive for wealthy settlers; there is always a long queue of millionaires on the waiting list. Should you win the lottery next week and decide to become a tax exile, you may find resident status is an elusive and protracted goal. For holiday visitors, though, the lower costs of some items, especially jewellery, alcohol, car hire and petrol, give Jersey that extra sparkle.

JERSEY TODAY

Partly because of its tax status, Jersey is a wealthy place, and its residents enjoy the good life in smart restaurants and yacht marinas, with the town of St Helier at its heart. Haute couture, fine jewels and expensive perfumes vie for the attention of shoppers keen for a tax-free bargain, as do restaurants and cafés serving delicious local specialities. Jersey has a policy of using only the freshest foods available, such as the home-grown Jersey Royal potatoes, and is renowned for its sophisticated take on cuisine.

Jersey hasn't lost its roots, however, and rejoices in its diversity of traditional crafts. Take home a beautiful piece of glass-ware or pottery as a gift and it's sure to be greatly appreciated. There's lots for families to do, too, ranging from new multi-media attractions, the island's famous zoo, sports centres and visits to fortifications, to sunbathing and beachcombing.

Whether you like beautiful landscapes and coast, traditional crafts, history or plenty of family fun, Jersey has the lot. Top this off with duty-free shopping and some particularly fine dining and the experience is complete.

◗ *One of Jersey's lovely beaches*

The best of Jersey

BEACHES

Jersey has gorgeous beaches (see pages 52–55). The eastern, western and southern edges have huge swathes of sand; the north coast has smaller, quieter ones. Some reveal rocks and reefs at low tide – which are great for rockpooling but not for swimming or water sports. Others are prized for surfing and sailing – be sure to respect safety signs and beachguards.

CHURCHES

Each of the parishes of Jersey has its own church. Many of them are handsome and surprisingly large buildings – interesting inside and out. Below is a short list of some you may like to see if you're passing. Many have interesting modern stained glass – Jersey airport, for instance, features in a window of St Peter's.

- **St Brelj's Church** Located in a gorgeous setting, St Brelade's church and its adjacent Fisherman's Chapel date from Norman times. Notice the wall paintings in the chapel.
- **St Helier's Church** The capital's parish church is named after the island's patron, who was beheaded by pirates. See the monument to gallant Major Peirson who died defending Jersey from the French in 1781.
- **St Matthew's Church** This church is also known as the Glass Church and is famous for its white glasswork by the Parisian artist René Lalique (1860–1945).
- **St Saviour's Church** Famous for the fact that Lillie Langtry (see page 14) was born in the rectory, married in the church and is buried in the graveyard.

CASTLES & FORTRESSES

For over a thousand years, the Channel Islands have been subjected to invasion, or threats of invasion. All around the coastline the islanders have tried to ward off the danger by building fortresses and watch-towers. Among Jersey's best are:

🔺 *Jersey is famed for its huge swathes of sand*

- **Elizabeth Castle**   Set high on a tiny island just off St Helier.
- **Mont Orgueil Castle**   A landmark near Gorey village in Grouville.
- **Kempt Tower**   On the west coast in St Ouen's Bay.
- **Grève de Lecq Barracks**   Houses the North Coast Visitor Centre.

THE OTHER CHANNEL ISLANDS...
Guernsey
Guernsey is only a little over half Jersey's size, and though more densely populated, it feels quieter and more intimate. It has lots of charm, especially along its pretty, cliff-fringed southern coastline and in its capital, St Peter Port, as well as excellent historic sights and shops.

Alderney, Sark & Herm
Alderney, next in size, is very much smaller and less populous. Geography keeps it free of mass tourism, so it appeals to lovers of peace and quiet,

bird-watching and open spaces. Its coastline, fringed by fortresses, sandy beaches and rugged cliffs, is uniquely memorable. In the evenings, it is a sociable place with convivial pubs and community life.

Sark's glorious scenery and winsome feudal customs make it an instant hit with visitors. You can easily see the island on a day trip, as thousands do, but it's even better if you stay at one of its excellent hotel-restaurants. Beaches are small and quite difficult to reach, and there are no organized attractions or nightlife. **Herm** is totally unspoilt and you can while away many hours on the sand dunes, its lovely shell beach, or following the amazing cliff top walks.

◆ *Exploring Sark by horse-drawn cart*

RESORTS
Places under the sun

St Helier
seat of parliament

St Helier's waterfront, formerly a dreary area of commercial wharfs and ferry terminals dominated by a power station, continues to undergo a massive refurbishment. There are many new public spaces, fountains and facilities being created. The attractive buildings housing the Occupation Tapestry and Maritime Museum are a good start. Across the sweeping, sheltered bay of St Aubin is Elizabeth Castle, a Tudor fortress, romantically floodlit at night.

Liberation Square, focus of post-World War II jubilation, makes a natural starting point. Nearby is the colourful **Steam Clock**. In the streets behind you'll discover the town's true character – quaint old shop-fronts and names in Norman French. Visit the delightful old market and historic **Royal Square**, where one of the Commonwealth's oldest parliaments sits. The immaculate gardens of **Howard Davis Park** offer a peaceful retreat from the traffic.

Several of Jersey's best museums, run by the Jersey Museums Service, have a combined ticketing scheme – excellent value if you visit more than a couple. Passport Savers can be purchased at any participating ticket office or from your holiday representative.

THINGS TO SEE & DO
Elizabeth Castle ★ ★ ★
The unmissable causeway fortress in St Aubin's Bay dates from the 1590s, and was named after Elizabeth I. History exhibitions and the Royal Jersey Militia Museum are inside. Access on foot (low tide only) or by an amphibious vehicle dubbed the 'duck' (extra charge). Behind the castle is the Hermitage, a 12th-century chapel dedicated to St Helier, who was murdered by axe-wielding pirates. ❸ St Aubin's Bay ❶ 01534 633300 ❻ Open 10.00–18.00 (mid-Mar–Oct) ❶ Admission charge, difficult access for visitors with disabilities

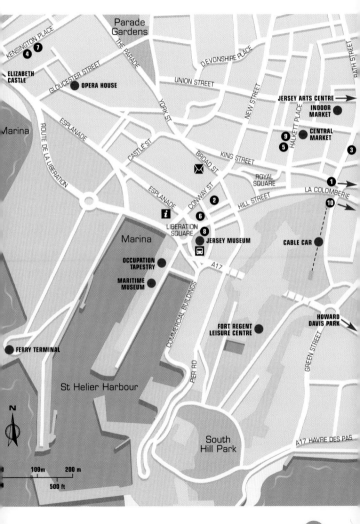

Parade Gardens

KENSINGTON PLACE

❹ ❼

ELIZABETH CASTLE

GLOUCESTER STREET

THE PARADE

DEVONSHIRE PLACE

UNION STREET

OPERA HOUSE

Marina

ESPLANADE

ROUTE DE LA LIBERATION

YORK ST

CASTLE ST

BROAD ST

NEW STREET

JERSEY ARTS CENTRE →

INDOOR MARKET ●

HALKETT PLACE

❾ CENTRAL MARKET

❺

❸

KING STREET

ROYAL SQUARE

ESPLANADE

CONWAY ST

❷

❶ →

LA COLOMBERIE

❿ →

HILL STREET

LIBERATION SQUARE

❻

❽

JERSEY MUSEUM

CABLE CAR ●

Marina

OCCUPATION TAPESTRY

MARITIME MUSEUM

A17

COMMERCIAL BUILDINGS

HOWARD DAVIS PARK

FORT REGENT LEISURE CENTRE ●

GREEN STREET

FERRY TERMINAL ●

PIER RD

St Helier Harbour

N

South Hill Park

A17 HAVRE DES PAS

100m   200 m

500 ft

Fort Regent ★★

The curious golf-ball structure towering over St Helier's harbour houses a massive sports, leisure and entertainment complex in the grounds of a 19th-century fort. It also has a 2000-seat concert hall. Learn the history of the fort on a guided tour, and don't miss the signalling tower and the rampart views. ⓐ Harbour ❶ 01534 500200 ⓛ Opening times vary according to activity or event ❶ Admission free; pay as you play

⬤ A visit to Elizabeth Castle is a must

Jersey Museum ★★★

An award-winning multi-media presentation of Jersey's history and culture, with an art gallery and excellent catering facilities. Interesting sections on Lillie Langtry (Edward VII's glamorous mistress), and a restored merchant's house on the top floor. **ⓐ** The Weighbridge **ⓘ** 01534 633300 **ⓛ** Open 10.00–17.00 (mid-Mar–Oct); 10.00–16.00 (winter) **ⓘ** Admission charge

Maritime Museum ★★★

In the same attractive, waterfront premises as the Occupation Tapestry (see below), this excellent museum has many entertaining 'hands-on' ways to learn about tides, winds, cleats and sails. A must for sailing enthusiasts. **ⓐ** New North Quay **ⓘ** 01534 811043 **ⓛ** Open 10.00–17.00 (mid-Mar–Oct); 10.00–16.00 (winter) **ⓘ** Admission charge

Occupation Tapestry ★★★

The Occupation Tapestry was an ambitious project to commemorate the 50th anniversary of the Liberation and it was finally completed in 1995. The whole island was involved with each parish contributing one of the dozen panels depicting Jersey's wartime experiences. It contains over seven million stitches. Informative video and gift shop. **ⓐ** New North Quay **ⓘ** 01534 811043 **ⓛ** Open 10.00–17.00 (mid-Mar–Oct); 10.00–16.00 (winter) **ⓘ** Admission charge

RESTAURANTS & PUBS (see map on page 21)

As you might expect, St Helier has the island's widest choice of eating and drinking places, including large and reliable chain restaurants, such as **Pizza Express** and **McDonald's**. Several pubs offer regular live music in the evenings.

The Admiral Wine & Ale House £ **❶** One of St Helier's best-known haunts for inexpensive lunchtime food, decent bitter and dominoes. **ⓐ** St James Street **ⓘ** 01534 730095 **ⓛ** Open from 18.00 for evening meals

La Bastille £ ❷ Popular wine-bar serving a wide range of dishes at very reasonable prices. Daily specials and good seafood. ❸ 4 Wharf Street ❶ 01534 874059 🕒 Open noon–16.00

Blue Fish Café ££ ❸ Trendy informal eatery in central St Helier, specializing in pasta, pizza and brochettes. Outdoor seating during summer, cosy in winter. ❸ 8–10 West Centre ❶ 01534 767186 ❶ Popular, so book in advance

Candlelight Restaurant ££ ❹ This restaurant serves French and English cuisine and fine wines in traditional surroundings. Part of the Revere Hotel, a 17th- century coach house. Walking distance of the Esplanade. ❸ Kensington Place ❶ 01534 611111

La Capannina £££ ❺ An accomplished Italian restaurant, highly acclaimed for traditional cuisine using local produce. Good wines too. Smart and formal. ❸ 65–67 Halkett Place ❶ 01534 734602 🕒 Open Mon–Sat ❶ Book ahead

Chambers £ ❻ A younger sibling of the long-established Admiral, this popular pub appeals to a lively crowd, with regular music in the evenings. It has well-kept beers and good-value bar food. ❸ Mulcaster Street ❶ 01534 880432

Doran's Courtyard Bistro ££ ❼ An intimate ambience of warehouse windows, rustic beams and flagstone floors adds to the imaginative, eclectic fare served here. ❸ Kensington Place ❶ 01534 734866 🕒 Open Mon–Sat ❶ Book ahead – it's very popular with the locals

Jersey Museum Brasserie £ ❽ This excellent brasserie is open to non-museum visitors and serves sophisticated snacks and cakes.

ⓐ The Weighbridge ☎ 01534 510069 ⏱ Open museum hours and for evening dining from 18.30

🍴 **KG's Diner** £ ❾ A clean, comfortable, welcoming place to enjoy some of Jersey's best fish and chips, plus great steaks and snacks. Friendly service and wines by the glass. Good value. ⓐ 90–92 Halkett Place, opposite Jersey Library ☎ 01534 721395

🍴 **Olive Branch** ££ ❿ An eclectic menu includes homemade pastas and the finest Italian sauces. Good wine list with a plentiful number of Italian wines. Light, modern décor and friendly staff. ⓐ 35–39 Colomberie ☎ 01534 615993 ⏱ Open Mon–Sat

NIGHTLIFE

Despite its size, Jersey has a wide range of entertainment. Much of it centres on St Helier, where pubs and clubs keep going until the small hours. In particular, the area surrounding the bus station is where many nightlife venues can be found. Check the *Jersey Evening Post* to see what is on. Nightlife tends to be busiest during the summer months. You can choose from a military band playing in **Howard Davis Park** to a rock band in **Chambers Pub**, or visit one of St Helier's nightclubs.

If your tastes are more high-brow, see what is on at the **Jersey Opera House**. This beautifully restored 600-seat theatre in Gloucester Street holds performances every week of touring musicals and plays. Also check out **St James's** and the **Jersey Arts Centre**, smaller theatres hosting classical recitals, plays and art exhibitions. St Helier also offers cinema; head for **Cineworld** on the waterfront for the latest releases.

Outside St Helier, nightlife is rather quieter. There are many community clubs offering everything from bridge to Latin, Ballroom, sequence and Egyptian dance classes. Some hotels, including the **Merton Hotel** and **Hotel de Normandie** in St Saviour provide entertainment and are open to non-residents.

St Clement & Grouville
inns and sands

Once free of St Helier's suburban tentacles, the hinterland of these south-eastern parishes consists of open farmland and proper villages boasting rustic inns and churches. The seigneurial manor of Samarès and its impressive portfolio of visitor attractions is a major draw. So too is the coastal village of Gorey, and the prehistoric burial mound at La Hougue Bie.

When you glimpse the beach at low tide, you'll see why the dramatic sea views along this part of Jersey's coastline are so popular – its amazing rock formations are exposed. The grassy hillock of **Green Island** is a particularly scenic spot, accessible at low tide; as a bathing beach, though, it is not so good. Choose your spot carefully and watch the warning signs.

As if those deadly reefs were not enough of a deterrent to invaders of the past, a string of fortress towers guards the shore. Round the headland of La Rocque, a fine belt of continuous sheltered sand lines the Royal Bay of Grouville, fringed by oyster beds, and the Royal Jersey Golf Club (club members only).

Take a drive along the coastal road past **St Clement's Bay** at low tide to see a strange lunar seascape of exposed reefs and rocks. It's particularly dramatic in morning light, so bring your camera. There are free parking places at intervals. Take care if you walk along the beach – the incoming tide moves extremely fast and can be dangerous.

THINGS TO SEE & DO
La Hougue Bie ★★
Deep in rural seclusion stands a 12 m (40 ft) mound pierced by a mysterious passage entrance. This neolithic burial site dating back over 5000 years now has a modern-day visitor centre ⓐ Route de la Hougue Bie, Grouville ⓣ 01534 853823 ⓛ Open 10.00–17.00 (Mar–Oct) ❶ Admission charge

Jersey Pottery ★★★

This family-run pottery makes an enjoyable day out. Watch ceramics being thrown, fired and painted by skilled artists or have a go at painting your own design. Splendid brasseries and restaurants (see page 29) ❷ Gorey Village ❶ 01534 851119 Ⓦ www.jerseypottery.com ● Showroom open Mon–Sat 09.00–17.30, Sun 10.00–17.30; no production Sat and Sun ❶ Admission free

Samarès Manor ★★★

This Norman seigneurial manor has a magnificent herb garden and plant nursery, crafts centre, tea gardens and fun farm. It offers demonstrations of woodturning and falconry; and guided tours of the house and the agricultural and carriage museum ❷ Inner Road, St Clement ❶ 01534 870551 ● Open Mon–Sat 10.00–17.00, closed Sun (Mar–Oct); tours of house Mon–Sat (additional charge) ❶ Admission charge

⬤ *La Hougue Bie, the neolithic burial site*

RESTAURANTS & PUBS

Jersey's south-east corner rejoices in several superb restaurants with moderate prices. It's worth working up an appetite if you're heading to this part of the island to eat.

◆ *Nearly 8 km (5 miles) of sand lines Grouville Bay*

Borsalino Rocque ££ A large, popular place, smart but friendly, with a huge menu. Book ahead for the conservatory. Lunches are moderate; dinners pricier. Disco dancing some evenings. ⓐ La Grande Route des Sablons, Grouville ⓣ 01534 852111 ⓛ Open Wed–Mon for lunch and evening meals, closed Tues

Green Island ££ Occupies a prime location overlooking the dramatic coastline of St Clement's Bay. Modest price-tags yet very interesting cooking (the owner is a celebrated Jersey restaurateur). Terrace tables. ⓐ Green Island, St Clement ⓣ 01534 857787 ⓛ Open Tues–Sat for lunch and evening meals, and Sun lunchtime, closed Mon

Jersey Pottery Restaurants £££ After much-deserved praise in several top food guides, these three restaurants which include a gastro pub and a café are now just as prestigious as the pottery. ⓐ Gorey Village, Grouville ⓣ 01534 850850 ⓦ www.jerseypottery.com ⓛ Opening times vary; check website or telephone for details

Pembroke £ Welcoming pub drawing visitors and locals for good-value food at lunchtime and in the evenings. ⓐ Grouville Coast Road, Grouville ⓣ 01534 855756 ⓛ Open daily all year

Secret Garden £ A popular daytime stop for cream teas and lunches. Licensed restaurant with daily specials and family favourites. Seafood is a speciality. ⓐ Gorey Common, Grouville ⓣ 01534 852999 ⓛ Open summer Wed–Mon 11.00–22.00 for late breakfast, lunch and evening meals, closed Tues

Village Bistro ££ An innovative menu that has become known on Jersey's gastronomic scene. Local produce is used to good effect in appetizing modern dishes. Set menus represent excellent value. ⓐ Gorey Village, Grouville ⓣ 01534 853429 ⓛ Open Tues–Sat for lunch and evening meals, and Sun lunchtimes, closed Mon

St Martin & Trinity
scaling the heights

Jersey's north-east parishes encompass the island's highest point, and some of its prettiest and most rural scenery. North of Gorey is a series of quiet, sandy bays – safe and unpolluted. Along the rugged northern shore, cliffs soar to a height of 120 m (400 ft) above the picturesque fishing harbours of Rozel and Bouley Bay. Inland, a web of secretive country lanes conceals dignified and prosperous-looking farmsteads.

One of these, **Les Augrès Manor**, now hosts the world-famous zoo set up by the late Gerald Durrell. Other popular sights in this part of Jersey are **Mont Orgeuil Castle** in Gorey, and the exotic, riotously colourful blooms of the **Eric Young Orchid Foundation**. The massive breakwater at **St Catherine's Bay** provides a popular pier for amateur fishermen.

More ominous is the rocky outcrop called **Geoffrey's Leap**, where condemned criminals were forced to plunge to their deaths in medieval times. The steep slopes behind **Bouley Bay** are the scene of an annual motorized hill-climbing championship. And, if the distant views of the Cotentin Peninsula in Normandy prove tempting, you can take a day-trip to France from Gorey Harbour (you will need your passport).

THINGS TO SEE & DO
Eric Young Orchid Foundation ★★
Green-fingered visitors beat a path through tiny lanes to these exotic hothouses where the lifetime's work of an orchid addict can be seen. High summer is not the best time to visit, but there are gorgeous flowers all year round in an astonishing range of shapes and colours. A wonderful experience. ❸ Victoria Village, Trinity ☎ 01534 861963 🕙 Open Wed–Sat 10.00–16.00 all year ❶ Admission charge

Gorey Village ★★
The picturesque cluster of harbour cottages dwarfed by Jersey's oldest castle makes a classic photo opportunity. Besides excellent restaurants,

shops, crafts and pubs, Gorey boasts several first-rate sights and overlooks a magnificent beach. More good beaches and pretty countryside lie nearby. Needless to say, it is popular in high season.

Jersey Zoo ★★★

The late Gerald Durrell's imaginative sanctuary and breeding centre has won many awards for its ground-breaking contribution to wildlife conservation. Rare species are rescued from the brink of extinction, and reintroduced to the wild. An informative, entertaining and inspiring place with a friendly, direct approach to visitors. The **Café Dodo** is a good bet for lunch or afternoon tea. ⓐ Les Augrès Manor, Trinity ⓣ 01534 860000 ⓛ Open daily 09.30–18.00 (summer); 10.00–17.00 (winter, except Christmas Day) ⓘ Admission charge

Little Loft Gallery & Turnery ★

Mick Renouf's beautifully handturned vases, bowls and goblets, mostly using native hardwoods, are displayed in this farmhouse gallery. ⓐ Brabant Farm, Rue de Brabant, Trinity ⓣ 01534 863674 ⓛ Open by appointment only ⓘ Admission free

Mont Orgeuil Castle ★★★

This splendid fortress has dominated Grouville Bay and Gorey Village since the 13th century, and is in remarkable condition. Exhibitions inside recount its history. Lovely rampart views. ⓐ Gorey, St Martin ⓣ 01534 853292

◒ *Rainforest flora at the Orchid Foundation*

🕐 Open daily 10.00–18.00 (Mar–Oct); Sat–Sun 10.00–18.00 (winter)
ⓘ Admission charge

Pallot Heritage Steam Museum ★

Steam engines, farm machinery, theatre organs and other bygones. Occasional steam train rides and special events. ❸ Rue de Bechet, Trinity
❶ 01534 865307 🕐 Open Mon–Sat 10.00–17.00, closed Sun (Apr–Oct)
ⓘ Admission charge

Queen's Valley Reservoir ★

The quiet reservoir of Queen's Valley, inland from Gorey, is also a nature reserve. The pathways leading round its edges make a gentle 1-km

⬤ *Leopard taking it easy at Jersey Zoo*

(2-mile) stroll. Take a picnic with you, or combine a walk with a visit to the nearby Jersey Pottery (see page 27) and its excellent brasserie/restaurants. There are additional car parks at either end of the reservoir.

RESTAURANTS & PUBS

Château La Chaire £££ This luxury hotel-restaurant occupies a beautiful and secluded spot near the tip of the island. It's an elegant place, so book ahead and dress up. Cooking is ambitious 'modern British', and very fish oriented. The oak-panelled restaurant has a conservatory extension. Dining on the terrace in summer. ⓐ Rozel Bay, St Martin ☎ 01534 863354

Drive Inn BBQ £ Popular with families for its generous helpings of chargrilled meat and fish served on a flower-decked terrace or in Western-style wagons. Self-service salad bar – eat as much as you like. ⓐ Gorey Coast Road, St Martin ☎ 01534 851266 🕘 Open May–Sept

Frère de Mer £££ Sitting at the top of Rozel Bay, the 'Frère' is a seafood haven, perfect for special occasion meals. Booking required. ⓐ Rozel Bay, St Martin ☎ 01534 861000 🕘 Open Tues–Sun for lunch and Tues–Sat for evening meals

Gardener's Tearoom and Restaurant £ Good wholesome family food served in the courtyard during the summer. Dishes such as local fish, pasta and exotic salads are prepared fresh on the premises. Delicious homemade cakes, bread and cream teas. ⓐ Ransoms Garden Centre, Grande Route de Faldouet, St Martin ☎ 01534 853668 🕘 Open Tues–Sun for lunch

Royal St Martin £ Renowned for its excellent bar food, this landmark village pub in the centre of St Martin also has a separate restaurant. Good real ales. Families welcome. ⓐ Grande Route de Faldouet, St Martin ☎ 01534 851098 🕘 Open daily for lunch, and Mon–Sat for evening meals

◔ *Mont Orgeuil Castle, Gorey*

Rozel Bay and Upstairs Restaurant £ A cosy seaside pub serving much-acclaimed food, particularly fish. Lunchtime fare is more traditional and less expensive, but the dinner fare is exceptional. Gardens and pub games. Children welcome. ⓐ Rozel Bay, St Martin ❶ 01534 863438 ❶ Booking recommended in high season

Suma's ££ This attractive venture offers discerning palates a chance to try first-class Mediterranean cooking at affordable prices. Under the same management as **Longueville Manor** (see page 50), Suma's has an airy upstairs dining-room, simple but stylish, over-looking Gorey Harbour. Good-value set lunches, an in-house bakery and a good wine list. Children welcome. ⓐ Gorey Hill, St Martin ❶ 01534 853291 ⓛ Open daily

St John & St Mary
rugged coastline

Cliff paths stretch along Jersey's scenic northern headlands, offering beautiful but taxing walks. There isn't much sand between Bonne Nuit Bay and Grève de Lecq, but energetic walkers can explore many minor natural features, such as the Wolf's Caves or the Devil's Hole. Take care with cliffs and tides and watch out for warning signs.

This rugged coastline, some of it is National Trust land, is best explored on foot, as the roads do not run by the sea. A blaze of wildflowers can be seen in spring and early summer and the area is a haunt of rare birds. It isn't always quiet, though – isolated headlands sometimes reverberate to the sounds of motorcycle scrambling or rifle shooting, and there are

⬥ *Enjoy the wonderful views from Jersey's north coast footpaths*

seasonal flickers of nightlife if you are out after hours at Grève de Lecq and Wolf's Caves.

There are a few small prehistoric sites, including tumuli dating from around 3500 BC. **L'Ile Agois** was once an islet hermitage and can be reached at low tide. The hinterland is quiet and agricultural, scattered with fine examples of domestic architecture. For more information on this part of the island it is a good idea to visit the **North Coast Visitor Centre**, housed in the Napoleonic barracks at Grève de Lecq.

⬤ *Few roads but many paths stretch along Jersey's scenic northern headlands*

For a closer look at some of Jersey's traditional farmhouses visit such tourist attractions as **La Mare Vineyards**. Another fine building, **The Elms**, is the Jersey National Trust HQ. Most imposing of all is **St John's Manor**, a classically proportioned house open occasionally for charity events.

THINGS TO SEE & DO
La Mare Vineyards ★

Jersey's only commercial vineyards were planted in 1972 in the grounds of a fine 18th-century farmhouse. It produces in the region of 30–40,000 bottles of wine per season, along with its renowned cider and calvados (apple brandy). La Mare also produces preserves, mustards, fudge, traditional black butter and chocolates in its estate kitchens. Video and exhibitions. Tastings and produce on sale. Adventure playground for the children. ⓐ St Mary ① 01534 481178 ⓦ www.lamarevineyards.com ⓛ Open Mon–Sat 10.00–17.00 (Mar–Oct) ⓘ Admission charge

North Coast Visitor Centre ★

Housed in the neat, symmetrical buildings of a 19th-century Napoleonic-era barracks, this National Trust-owned visitor centre has displays and literature on history, footpaths and wildlife. ⓐ Grève de Lecq, St Mary ① 01534 483193 ⓛ Open Tues–Sat 11.00–17.00, and Sun 14.00–17.00 (May–Sept) ⓘ Admission free

RESTAURANTS & PUBS

Teashops and good-value snacks in pubs dominate the eating scene here, but don't expect anything very elaborate. Evening restaurants are in short supply.

The Buttery Restaurant and Tearooms £ The tearooms attached to La Mare Vineyards are a pleasant place for a snack, with home-baked cakes and tables in the garden in fine weather. You may be able to taste some home produce here, including cider or perhaps even Calvados. ⓐ Rue de la Hougue Mauger, St Mary ① 01534 481178 ⓛ Open Mon–Sat 10.00–17.00 (Mar–Oct) ⓘ Admission charge

Les Fontaines Tavern £ Location is one of this old granite pub's selling points as it has spectacular ocean views. Inside, it has lots of character – inglenooks, ship's timber beams and an ancient cider press. Randall's ales and inexpensive bar food served at lunchtime and dinner. Children's play area. ⓐ Route du Nord, St John ⓣ 01534 862707 ⓛ Open daily 11.00–23.00

St Mary's Country Inn £ One of the best examples of a Jersey speciality – the family-friendly country pub. Civilized and welcoming, it offers a hearty range of lunchtime and evening food. Family conservatory room (no smoking) and tables outside for al fresco summer dining. ⓐ St Mary ⓣ 01534 481561 ⓛ Open daily 10.00–23.30

● *Fruits of the sea tempt gourmets to indulge*

◯ *The popular family beach at Grève de Lecq*

St Ouen
blooms in the breeze

St Ouen (pronounced 'won') is Jersey's largest parish. It makes up
the north-west corner of the island, a varied and beautiful stretch of
striking coastline and quiet farmland. Much is still uncultivated and it
is good place for walkers and nature-lovers. Coastal paths follow most
of the shore, partly on breezy clifftops, partly beside peaceful dunes.
There are some dangers on this exposed Atlantic seaboard, though,
so watch out for warning signs.

St Ouen boasts a large number of visitor attractions, though few merit more than a 'see if passing' rating. Many are clustered around **L'Etacq** and **St Ouen's Bay**. If you're keen on wildlife visit the **Kempt Tower** to learn more about Jersey's flora and fauna, or perhaps take part in a guided walk through the reedbeds and lagoons behind St Ouen's Bay.

Grève de Lecq and **Plémont Bay** are two of Jersey's most appealing smaller beaches, while the giant 8 km (5 mile) strand of St Ouen's Bay attracts surfers. Inland, the manor and church of St Ouen hark back to feudal times.

It's tempting to put your foot down if you are driving on the long straight road behind St Ouen's Bay. **La Route des Mielles** is one of the few stretches on Jersey where this is possible. Be careful if you're walking across this road – especially with young children. If you are driving, remember the island's speed limit is only 65 km/h (40 mph).

THINGS TO SEE & DO
Battle of Flowers Museum ★
A display of floats from Jersey's colourful annual parade, which usually takes place in August. Many of the award-winning floats were hand-made by museum founder Florence Bechelet. Taped commentary.
ⓐ Mont des Corvées, St Ouen ☎ 01534 482408 🕒 Open daily 10.00–17.00 (Easter–Oct) ❶ Admission charge

Bouchet Agateware Pottery ★
A unique and secret process developed by founder Tony Bouchet is behind the stunning marbled clay pieces created in this tiny pottery. Visit the showroom and find out more. ⓐ Rue des Marettes, St Ouen ☎ 01534 482345 🕒 Open daily 09.00–17.00 (summer), limited opening times in winter ❶ Admission free

Jersey Pearl ★
Simulated and cultured pearl jewellery is on show and sale here, alongside other precious and semi-precious gems and watches. Find out what

the largest pearl in the world looks like. Workshop demonstrations and exhibitions. Tearooms and gift shops. ❸ North End Five Mile Road, St Ouen (Also at Jersey airport and Gorey Pier shop) ❶ 01534 862137 ❺ Open 10.00–17.30 (summer); 10.00–16.30 (winter) ❶ Admission free

Kempt Tower ★

The stumpy Martello tower at the north end of St Ouen's Bay houses a visitor centre (complete with video theatre) dedicated to Jersey's natural

● *Windsurfing at St Ouen's Bay*

history. Nearby are the **Frances Le Sueur Centre** (an environmental information and education base which has been instrumental in restoring the island's floral habitat including the protection of orchids) and **Les Mielles**, a nature reserve that is home to many wild flowers and butterflies. 🄰 St Ouen's Bay 🄱 01534 483651 🄲 Open Tues–Sun 14.00–17.00 (Apr–Oct); free guided nature walks on Thurs in summer 🄸 Admission free

Picnic spots

The clifftop walk between Grève de Lecq and L'Etacq offers some panoramic views. **Plémont Point** is a good spot for birdwatching: auks, fulmars and shags build nests on the cliffs, while pipits and linnets flit across the open heathland behind. On a fine day, the 14th-century ruins of **Grosnez Castle**, 60 m (200 ft) above sea level, makes a scenic vantage point. Further round the headland, by the water's edge, is the rock spire **Le Pinacle**. A sea cave is exposed at low tide and wild flowers carpet the treeless expanses of **Les Landes** in spring.

RESTAURANTS & PUBS

Moulin de Lecq £ The watermill theme of this delightful place makes it instantly appealing; see the machinery gears turning as you order drinks at the bar. Log fires, real ales and generous bar food add to the olde worlde character. Children's playground and al fresco dining in the summer. 🄰 Grève de Lecq, St Ouen 🄱 01534 482818 🄲 Open daily for lunch and evening meals

The Snow Goose £ This pleasant daytime tearoom opposite the parish hall serves morning coffee, light lunches and cream teas. Adjoining is a large display of gifts and crafts. 🄰 St Ouen village 🄱 01534 484404 🄲 Open daily 10.00–17.00 (summer); Tues–Sat 10.00–17.00 (winter)

St Peter & St Brelade
subtropical gardens and beaches

St Peter is the first landfall for most visitors to Jersey – the island's airport is here. St Brelade, in the south-west corner, is one of the best-known and best-loved of Jersey's parishes. Meanwhile, St Brelade's Bay is the island's most attractive beach resort, basking amid palm-fringed gardens. It boasts of being the most southerly seaside town in the British Isles – a claim occasionally challenged by St Helier.

Though somewhat suburban in parts, both parishes have surprising swathes of unspoilt greenery. **St Peter's Valley** is one of Jersey's prettiest and greenest drives. With two separate stretches of coastline, St Peter offers access to Jersey's largest beaches and a variety of water sports

◆ St Brelade's Bay remains largely unspoilt

facilities. It also has one of Jersey's most ambitious attractions, 'The Living Legend', which includes The Jersey Experience (a re-creation of Jersey through the ages), adventure golf; and craft shops among its many attractions.

● *Sun and sand at St Brelade's Bay*

St Brelade capitalizes on one of Jersey's best family beaches. Glorious peaceful coves nestle between rocky headlands to either side, and rare wildlife haunts the open spaces behind. Beyond the fortified promontory of Noirmont, **St Aubin** has a distinctive salty character and is home to the prestigious Royal Channel Island Yacht Club and the nearby Shell Garden (see page 107). Other sporting interests are well catered for – there is tenpin bowling, several golf courses and a major leisure centre. It's a good place for energetic families, with lots of clifftop walks.

THINGS TO SEE & DO
Fisherman's Chapel ★★
The stippled frescoes in the early Norman chapel behind St Brelade's Bay look as though an agile leopard has had a shot at wall-painting with its paws. ❸ St Brelade's Bay ❶ Donations welcome

Jersey Lavender Farm ★★
Lavender is grown and harvested on the farm, and the oil is then extracted and blended into cosmetics and toiletries. Visit the farm, the distillery and, of course, the shop. A good time to visit is between early June and late July when you can see – and smell – the stunning swathes of lavender. ❸ Rue du Pont Marquet, St Brelade ❶ 01534 742933 ❷ Open Mon–Sun 10.00–17.00 (May–Sept) ❶ Admission charge

Jersey Motor Museum ★

Veteran and vintage cars, and a section on Jersey's steam railway.
ⓐ St Peter's Village ⓘ 01534 482966 ⓛ Open 10.00–17.00 (Apr–Oct)
ⓘ Admission charge

The Living Legend ★★★

One of Jersey's foremost attractions, The Living Legend village includes
a multi-media presentation of the island's story with many special
effects (known as The Jersey Experience). Housed within the same
complex of landscaped grounds and play areas is adventure golf, a
craft and shopping village, a restaurant, an ice-cream parlour and
a fudge factory. ⓐ La Rue du Petit Aleval, St Peter ⓘ 01534 485496
ⓛ Open daily 09.30–17.00 (Apr–Oct); Sat–Wed 10.00–17.00 (Mar and
Nov) ⓘ Admission charge

Le Moulin de Quétivel ★★

A well-restored 18th century watermill owned by the Jersey National
Trust. See the mill wheel in action and buy stone-ground flour.
ⓐ Mont Fallu, St Peter ⓛ Open Tues–Thurs 10.00–16.00 (May–Sept)
ⓘ 01534 745408 ⓘ Admission charge (free to worldwide National
Trust members)

Corbière Point is one of Jersey's most glorious yet rugged spots.
Head out here with your camera and watch as the lighthouse
becomes silhouetted against the sunset. At low tide you can walk
across to it on a rocky causeway, but check the tide tables first as
the rush of water can be extremely powerful and makes the area
particularly dangerous.

RESTAURANTS & PUBS

Stacks of choice to suit all pockets here, particularly near the popular
beaches of St Brelade, St Aubin and Portelet Bay. In addition to those
listed below, the smart hotels **The Atlantic** and **L'Horizon** have excellent,
if pricey, restaurants for a special treat.

The Victoria Pub, in rural St Peter's Valley

Old Court House Inn ££ A fine historic building right on the harbour front, as popular for the character of its interior and friendly service as for its excellent food and ales. You may remember it as the well-used backdrop to the 1980s *Bergerac* TV detective series. ❷ St Aubin's Harbour, St Brelade ❶ 01534 746433 ● Open daily for lunch and evening meals

Old Portelet Inn £ An excellent place for families, this converted farmhouse inn occupies a splendid location above Portelet Bay. Great-value bar food and ales and friendly service. There are outside tables and music some evenings. ❷ Portelet, St Brelade ❶ 01534 741899 ● Open Tues–Sun for lunch and evening meals

Smugglers Inn £ Down by the beach at Ouaisné, this traditional family pub serves wholesome lunches and dinners, popular after a day on the beach. ❷ Ouaisné, St Brelade ❶ 01543 741510 ● Open daily for lunch and evening meals, closed Sun evening in winter

The Star £ A friendly village pub offering terrific value. No food served at present but has plans to do so in the future. ❷ St Peter's Village ❶ 01543 485556

Victoria Pub £ Popular family pub in the rural centre of the island. ❷ St Peter's Valley ❶ 01534 485498 ● Open Tues–Sat for lunch and evening meals, plus Sun lunchtime for traditional roasts

CORBIÈRE WALK

Since 1936 when the railway station at St Aubin was destroyed by fire, the track used by the Jersey Railway has remained undeveloped. The line opened in 1870 linking St Helier with St Aubin on the opposite side of the bay. By 1884 it had been extended west to Corbière Lighthouse, which is one of Jersey's most photographed landmarks. After the fire, Jersey Railway ceased to operate. The route today provides an easy and popular walk, about 14 km (8 miles) there and back, through interesting and varied scenery. The round trip takes approximately 3–4 hours, though there are good bus services operating at both ends: buses nos. 12, 12a and 15 run from St Helier to St Aubin, while bus no. 12 returns from Corbière. In hot weather, it is best to wear a sunhat and take bottled water; binoculars are useful for birdwatching.

From **St Aubin's Harbour**, the main road turns inland at a junction marked '**Railway Walk Corbière**'. This path is the start of the track, which runs along the main road at first but gradually slips away into deep countryside. The first couple of miles after this is woodland. A little way along you cross under a road. Keep an eye out for rare wildlife such as the kingfisher and red squirrel.

Further on you approach a built-up area – **Les Quennevais** (pronounced 'Ken'evay'). The path leads under the busy main road before rising gently as you pass the Sports Centre. Further on, look to your right to see the edge of **La Moye Golf Course** and some school playing fields. You'll get glimpses of the **Blanches Banques** dunes and the sweep of **St Ouen's Bay**, too. For the following mile or so the route criss-crosses roads and lanes, leading you back into quieter wilderness.

At the end of the route you can see **Corbière Lighthouse**, which is particularly photogenic at sunset after a warm day. If the tide is out you can venture across the causeway, taking care not to be stranded later by the incoming tide.

St Lawrence & St Saviour
inland Jersey

You'll certainly find yourself travelling through these two central parishes at some stage. They suffer somewhat from their proximity to St Helier, with busy traffic routes and built-up areas, but inland these features are soon outstripped. St Lawrence has several interesting sights. The huge bay of St Aubin's is a fine, firm crescent of sand, if rather spoilt by the busy highway running directly behind.

Two of the most interesting attractions in St Lawrence are the German Underground Hospital, an amazing complex of underground tunnels constructed in the last war, and the Hamptonne Country Life Museum, run by the Jersey Museums Service and occupying one of the finest farmhouses in the parish.

As you drive around, you'll see other impressive examples of Jersey's vernacular (or domestic) architecture too. Several of these are looked after by the National Trust for Jersey (though not open to the public). Look out for Morel Farm, and Le Rat Cottage.

A couple of churches are worth visiting, too: Millbrook's Glass Church is decorated with astonishing Lalique glasswork, while St Saviour's Church is the last resting place of the dashing Emilie Charlotte le Breton, better known as Lillie Langtry. Nearby, have a look at the imposing residence of the Lieutenant Governor, the Queen's representative on Jersey.

● *War relic, the German Underground Hospital*

THINGS TO SEE & DO
German Underground Hospital ★ ★ ★

This graphic evocation of the Occupation period is set in a complex of tunnels dug by forced labour and equipped as a hospital for German casualties. Fascinating reconstructions and film footage.
➋ Meadowback, St Lawrence ☏ 01534 863442 ◷ Open 10.00–18.00 (Feb–Dec) ❶ Admission charge

The Glass Church ★ ★

The exterior of St Matthew's church near Coronation Park is unremarkable, but it contains wonderful artefacts in moulded white glass made by the French artist René Lalique which date from 1932. The main doors are glass, as is the font, the altar cross and there is an exquisite set of Art Deco angels.
➋ Milbrook, St Lawrence ☏ 01534 502864 ◷ Open Sun–Fri 09.00–18.00 (19.00 in winter), closed Sat ❶ Donations welcome

Hamptonne Country Life Museum ★ ★

An enjoyable folk museum comprising reconstruction of Jersey's rural heritage over the past 300 years, craft demonstrations, a nature trail and farm animals.
➋ La Rue de la Patente, St Lawrence ☏ 01534 863955 ◷ Open daily 10.00–17.00 (Apr–Oct) ❶ Admission charge

◓ The Glass Church

Jersey Goldsmiths ★★

This widely promoted attraction is featured on many sightseeing tours. Set in the parish of St Lawrence in Lion Park, where you can picnic in the attractive landscaped gardens or buy a light snack at the on-site restaurant. Exhibitions include designing with precious stones, the history of gold, and celebrity memorabilia. You have an opportunity to watch craftsmen at work, and see a huge range of costume jewellery, much of it plated in 18-carat gold. Repairs and adjustments carried out. Garden terrace restaurant. ⓐ La Rue des Varvots, St Lawrence ⓣ 01534 482098 ⓛ Open 10.00–17.00 ⓘ Admission free

RESTAURANTS & PUBS

British Union £ Right in the centre of the island, this popular roadside pub serves simple bar food. Pleasant service. Games room and playhouse. ⓐ Main Road, St Lawrence ⓣ 01534 861070 ⓛ Open daily for lunch and evening meals (except Sun)

The Hamptonne Café £ The Country Life Museum's attractive café will organize a picnic for you to eat in the meadow, and also serves snacks and teas available throughout the day. Typical Jersey recipes on offer. ⓐ La Rue de la Patente, St Lawrence ⓣ 01534 862698 ⓛ Open Apr–Oct

Longueville Manor £££ One of Jersey's most celebrated restaurants in a country house hotel. Smart and formal but very comfortable, with a courteous, welcoming service. Fine gastronomy menus using homegrown fruit, vegetables and herbs. Vegetarian options. ⓐ Longueville Road, St Saviour ⓣ 01534 725501

Ming's Dynasty ££ There are three branches of this popular Chinese restaurant on Jersey (the others are in St Helier and Gorey Village), all producing reliable, well-prepared oriental classics, incorporating fresh local seafood. ⓐ Sandybrook Lane, St Lawrence ⓣ 01534 888682 ⓛ Open daily at 18.00

Beach tour

Jersey tilts southwards like a solar panel, which means it catches plenty of sunshine. The largest beaches lie along its eastern, western and southern sides (see map on pages 12–13). The cliff-edged northern coast has much smaller beaches, though these include some of the prettiest on the island. This brief coastal tour leads clockwise from St Helier.

St Aubin's Bay A huge arc of gentle sand, so flat and smooth that it was used as an aircraft runway before the war. St Aubin's pretty houses and quayside bistros rise from a harbour full of smart pleasure craft. There's a large water sports complex at La Haule near St Aubin, where windsurfing, waterskiing and sailing can be organized. Plenty of space to park.

Portelet Bay A pretty beach tucked into the steep Noirmont headland and bristling with German fortifications. Access to the beach is steep, down many steps (some through a large holiday village). Good headland walks and picnic spots.

Ouaisné Bay This sandy southerly continuation of St Brelade's Bay is much quieter than the main resort. Behind lies Ouaisné (pronounced 'Waynee') Common, an important conservation area (display boards in the car park tell you about agile frogs and creeping willow). Massive anti-tank defences constructed by the Germans act as a sea wall, but the bay is very beautiful, looking across to the wooded heights of Beauport and St Brelade. There are toilets for visitors with disabilities.

St Brelade's Bay One of the best beaches in the Channel Islands which has a distinctly Mediterranean feel. Despite its popularity, the lovely boardwalk setting remains largely unspoilt. There are plenty of resort facilities including trampolining and various water sports. Easy access, car parking, excellent restaurants and cafés, and subtropical gardens mean you can easily spend an entire day here. Beachguards patrol during the summer.

Beauport Just beyond St Brelade's, a charming little cove well worth tracking down for a quiet picnic or walk through brambly hills. Follow the lanes from the Fisherman's Chapel. Steep climb from car park.

Petit Port Another little cove near the scenic rocks of Corbière, pretty but exposed to the Atlantic. Sand and rock pools appear at low tide. Good walks on the gorse-covered headland.

St Ouen's Bay Jersey's largest and wildest beach, dramatic in storms and not advised for weak swimmers. Best known as a surfing beach, it is also popular with joggers and sandcar-racers. Behind the bay is a low-lying belt of dunes and salt marshes, an important conservation area. It also has beach kiosks, toilets and a beachguard in summer – watch for signs.

🔵 *St Brelade's Bay*

Plémont Bay Beyond the ruins of Grosnez Castle, the beach at Plémont Bay (also called Grève-au-Lançon) appears only at low tide and has some dangerous currents, but the flat golden stretches of sand are good for games and there are rock pools and waterfall caves to explore. Beachguards patrol here in summer. Steep steps lead down from a café. Lovely headland walks are available, with rare birds and flowers on the downs of Les Landes.

Grève de Lecq A beautiful bay of golden sand, popular with families and easily reached.

Bonne Nuit Bay St John's only stretch of sand is a pretty place protected by high cliffs, and shaded towards sundown. The fishing harbour gives it character (and good crab sandwiches!). A good stretch of firm sand is revealed at low tide, but it shelves quite steeply so take care with young children. Beach café but very limited parking. There are picturesque cliff walks all around.

Bouley Bay Famed as a diving and fishing centre, these clear waters offer safe bathing in the harbour area, but are quite steeply shelving. Steps from café. Steep access road and limited parking. The harbour pier makes a popular fishing spot.

Rozel Bay This delightful wooded bay has fishing village charm and plenty of good eating places. The sparkling sea is bobbing with boats at high tide, and a sandy beach is revealed at low water. Parking here can be difficult.

Fliquet Bay Mostly rocks and pebbles, but good for quiet walks and picnics. No facilities.

St Catherine's Bay Sheltered by a huge breakwater, this beach has a pebbly foreshore, but some sand at low tide, as well as a café and sailing club.

Archirondel Acclaimed for its clean water, the beach here is mostly shingle, but very pretty. Beach kiosk and toilets are available, as well as parking, with wooded walks behind the beach. The small neighbouring cove of **Havre de Fer** has a similarly rocky setting.

Anne Port This is a shingle and sand beach just north of the village of Gorey. It is easy to reach but parking is very limited. The rocky headland of Geoffrey's Leap (south) evokes an interesting tale of a criminal who survived his death-sentence plunge to the rocks below and was acquitted, but he volunteered to have another go to show how easy it was. Second time – not so lucky.

Royal Bay of Grouville The royal appendage was added by Queen Victoria, who gave it her seal of approval. With nearly 8 km (5 miles) of sand and open common behind, it is a marvellous space for beach games and safe bathing. The exclusive **Royal Jersey Golf Club** lies behind, along with a string of defensive towers. The **Gorey Watersports Centre** provides sailing, windsurfing, canoeing, etc. It is a popular sailing bay, and there are wading birds in winter.

St Clement's Bay Jagged reefs and rock pools stretch for miles at low tide here. Choose a parking place and admire the view for a while, but if you walk down to the beach itself, beware of dangerous tidal flows.

Green Island A safer beach with good sand and in a very pretty setting. There is an excellent restaurant; with parking and toilets. You can also walk out to the 'green island' at low tide to view neolithic remains.

Grève d'Azette Good firm sand at low tide, with rocky outcrops are to be found here. There is a ribbon development behind, and there is parking at intervals.

Havre des Pas St Helier's easterly town beach, rather spoilt by traffic and buildings but with good sand and a seawater pool.

North coast drive
day trip from St Ouen

This leisurely car itinerary explores Jersey's north coast, heading east from St Ouen and passing through the parishes of St Mary, St John, Trinity and St Martin. You could spend a day on this route, though driving non-stop it would only take about two hours. Drive carefully – some of the narrow roads are Green Lanes and have a maximum speed limit of just 24 km/h (15 mph). It's also worth taking your binoculars for the stunning views of the other islands and France.

THE ROUTE

Start at the car park of Jersey Pearl in St Ouen, turning right out of its exit on to the B64. Soon after, turn left where the sign says 'La Saline' and then right, to head along the sea wall. Stop the car briefly to admire the sweeping view behind you of St Ouen's Bay, the largest bay in the islands. At the end of this road turn left on to the B35 and follow it up the hairpin bend. Look out for the seafood van – it's well worth stopping to check the catch of the day. Take a sharp left on to the B55. Keep an eye out for Les Landes Race Course and Grosnez Castle ruins.

GROSNEZ

Dating from the 14th century, Grosnez is well protected by steep cliffs on three sides. The castle served as a refuge for the inhabitants when the island was raided, and some people say it is haunted. A cliff path walk starts here and winds its way along the entire north coast, while below lies La Baie de la Vielle; this point affords the best view of Guernsey and Sark. Continue along the B55 and head for Plémont. Turn left where the sign says 'C105 to Plemont Bay' and follow this road, finally stopping in the car park at the top. If you're feeling energetic, descend the steps to visit Plemont Bay, one of Jersey's hidden gems. Afterwards, double back to the crossroads and turn left towards Leoville. Turn left again on to the B65 and follow this road down to Grève de Lecq.

⬥ *Jersey's dramatic north coast, view towards Sorel*

GRÈVE DE LECQ

There are plenty of places to eat and drink at Grève de Lecq and there is a good beach, although it's not the best for swimming. The single-storey buildings on the hill behind the bay were built in the early 19th century and used by British troops as barracks. The 85 m (270 ft) mound guarding Grève de Lecq Bay has been fortified since prehistoric times and is now protected by the National Trust. From Grève de Lecq, carry along the B40 as it winds back inland. At the top of the hill you enter the Parish of St Mary – continue along the main road, passing the local school on the left. At the fork here turn left on to the C103, or La Grande Rue. On the way look out for signs to the nearby tourist attraction of La Mare Vineyards. Still on the C103, head for Devil's Hole.

Jersey's Green Lanes invite leisurely exploration

DEVIL'S HOLE

This curious spot is not as gruesome as it may sound. Devil's Hole is the name given to a blow hole which formed as the result of sea erosion, creating a hole in the roof of a cave. A local many years ago thought that they saw an image of a devil in the cave. Take care if you choose to go down to the cave, as the climb back is a real test. Continue on the road which takes you up to the cliffs again. After about a mile you pass through one of the most unspoilt and unpopulated parts of Jersey, Mourier Valley. At the bottom turn left on to Le Mont de la Barcelone, then straight on at Rue De Sorel. You are now in the parish of St John.

SOREL

Drive down as far as Sorel Point, the northern tip of Jersey. If you look out to sea, you'll see a reef between Jersey and Sark called the Paternosters. The name originates from the sailors who used to sail past the reef reciting The Lord's Prayer as they passed, anxious to avoid coming to grief. Continue along the C100. This is a particularly good stretch for views of the other islands and rugged coastline. Head towards Jersey's answer to the Eiffel Tower – the television mast – and at the end turn left. You can then either continue up to Wolf's Caves or turn right on to Rue de la Landes (you need good brakes for this road). Next turn left to head down to Bonne Nuit.

BONNE NUIT

Bonne Nuit Bay has many local stories attached to it. In the centre of the bay is a rock known as Le Cheval Guillaume, which used to be the site of a pagan pilgrimage; every Midsummer Day locals would take turns to row around the rock so as to avoid bad luck in the coming year. On leaving the bay turn left and head up the hill the other side (on the C98). At the top, turn left on to the B63, which becomes the C97 on entering the parish of Trinity. This is the highest point on the island. After a while turn left on to the C96, Rue de la Petite Falaise, to head down to Bouley Bay.

BOULEY BAY

There are various legends connected with Bouley Bay. Most notable is that of the Black Dog of Bouley Bay, a monstrous canine with terrifying saucer eyes that was said to roam around these lanes. The chances are that the tale was made up by local smugglers to frighten off interlopers while they brought their illicit goods ashore. The hill leading up from the bay is used for hill climb racing on occasional Bank Holidays. Head back up to the B31, Rue Es Picots, and turn left. The island's zoo is along this road, but as you really need a full day to cover the zoo properly, carry on for another half mile or so. At the next junction turn left at the C94, then left again following the sign to Rozel Bay; this road is the C93 and affords fantastic views. Head all the way down to Rozel.

ROZEL BAY

Rozel Bay, often described as a wooded amphitheatre, is the smallest and prettiest bay on the north coast. After Rozel, continue up the hill on the other side of the bay, then turn left on to the road signposted Fliquet and St Catherine's Bay, the B38, which leads into the parish of St Martin. Follow this road around before turning left again on to the B91, down to the junction for St Catherine's Bay.

ST CATHERINE'S BREAKWATER

At the crossroads turn left and follow the road to the end, to a small car park and excellent tea room. Take your time to stroll along the break-water to its end – the closest you can get to France without a passport! The giant breakwater at St Catherine's Bay on Jersey was one of the British Government's most embarrassing mistakes. After it was built at colossal expense in 1855 in response to threats of French attack, it was discovered no ships had a sufficiently shallow draught to use it!

A little way out from St Catherine's Breakwater you can see a cluster of three islands called the Ecrehous. During 18th-century elections, people who were known to support the minority political party were sometimes shipped out to the isles until the election was over. It is here that the tour ends.

St Peter Port, Guernsey
on the waterfront

In a Channel Island town beauty contest, St Peter Port would win hands down. The town focuses on the reclaimed waterfront. Ferries and fishing boats chug purposefully between the bristling jetties, while the halyards of the leisure boats clank in the breeze. St Peter Port is well worth a visit and is only an hour by ferry from Jersey. From the sea, the townscape of tall granite houses rising against wooded hillsides seems enmeshed in a cat's cradle of masts and maritime rigging. Exploring the picturesque old town takes you through steep cobbled streets linked by flights of steps, with plenty of good shops along the route.

THINGS TO SEE & DO
Castle Cornet ★★★
This 13th-century waterfront fortress is a major land and seamark containing historical, maritime and military museums. Built in King John's reign, it was last used for defence purposes by the Germans in World War II. At midday, red-coated retainers fire an artillery salute from the Royal Battery. ❸ Castle Emplacement ❶ 01481 726518 ❶ Open daily 10.00–17.00 (Apr–Oct) ❶ Admission charge

Guernsey Museum & Art Gallery ★★★
An excellent introduction to the history of the island from neolithic times. Audio-visual show and art gallery. Look out for the pretty bandstand and Victor Hugo's statue in the surrounding Victorian pleasure gardens. ❸ Candie Gardens ❶ 01481 726518 ❶ Open daily 10.00–17.00 (summer); 10.00–16.00 (winter) ❶ Admission charge

La Valette Underground Military Museum ★★
Housed in a series of German wartime tunnels, this award-winning display of occupation memorabilia is particularly atmospheric. ❸ La Valette ❶ 01481 722300 ❶ Open daily 10.00–17.00 (summer) ❶ Admission charge

THE ENGLISH CHANNEL

N

0   2 km
0   1 mile

Saline Bay

Cobo Bay

COB

ALBECQ

Vazon Bay

Perelle Bay

LE GELÉ

LIHOU ISLAND

Le Tricoteur   MONT SAINT

G

CASTEL

ERÉE

L'Erée Bay

ST SAVIOUR

LES BUTTES

Rocquaine Bay

ST PETER IN THE WOOD

Guernsey Woodcarvers   Strawberry Farm

Fort Grey   Guernsey Coppercraft

LONGFIRE

LA VILLIAZ

Portelet Bay

Le Coudré

Bruce Russell

PLEINMONT

LA BOUR

TORTEVAL

Hougue Anthan

TORTEVAL

LES LANDES

German Occu Mus

LES LAURENS

FOREST

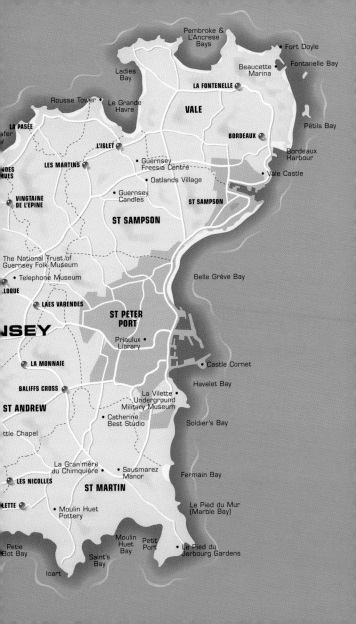

Hauteville House (Victor Hugo's home) ★★

The French writer lived as a political refugee in St Peter Port from 1855 to 1870, when he wrote his epic novel, *Les Miserables*. His astonishing taste in interior décor shows a resourceful streak. ◉ Hauteville ☎ 01481 721911 🕒 Open Mon–Sat noon–16.00 (Apr); Mon–Sat 10.00–16.00 (May–Sept) ❶ Conducted tours (45 min); admission charge

An excellent-value combined entrance ticket is available for three of Guernsey's most interesting historic sights: **Castle Cornet, Guernsey Museum** and **Fort Grey**.

RESTAURANTS & PUBS (see map opposite)

Absolute End ££ ❶ Award-winning seafood cooking on the seafront just north of St Peter Port. Good-value set lunches. Attentive, polished service. ◉ Longstore ☎ 01481 723822 🕒 Open daily for lunch and evening meals (times vary in winter)

Christie's ££ ❷ Stylish brasserie in the old town, overlooking the waterfront. Ideal for coffee and cakes, an early-evening drink, or a full meal. Specials with Oriental and Mediterranean flavours. Live jazz most evenings ◉ Le Pollet ☎ 01481 726624 🕒 Open daily for evening meals at 18.00

Da Nello ££ ❸ Intimate candlelit dining room offering classic Italian cooking and lots of seafood. Charcoal grills and pastas. Courteous, practised service. ◉ 46 Lower Pollet ☎ 01481 721552 🕒 Open daily for lunch and evening meals

Dix-Neuf Brasserie ££ ❹ Urbane bar-cum-brasserie in modern setting. Young friendly staff and lively music. Everything from chic Mediterranean specials to English breakfasts or sticky toffee pudding, but pleasant just for a drink too. ◉ 19 Commercial Arcade ☎ 01481 723455 🕒 Open daily for breakfast, lunch and evening meals (winter times can vary)

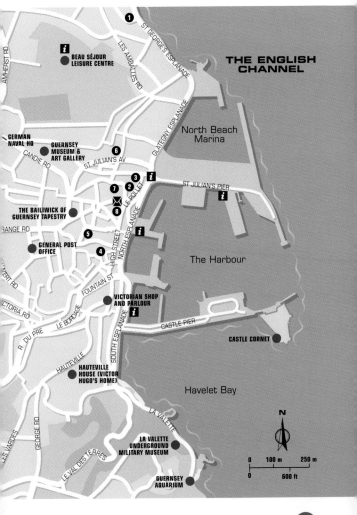

THE ENGLISH CHANNEL

BEAU SÉJOUR LEISURE CENTRE

North Beach Marina

GERMAN NAVAL HQ

GUERNSEY MUSEUM & ART GALLERY

ST JULIAN'S AV

AMHERST RD

LES AMBALLES RD

ST GEORGE'S ESPLANADE

GLATEGNY ESPLANADE

CANDIE RD

THE BAILIWICK OF GUERNSEY TAPESTRY

GRANGE RD

GENERAL POST OFFICE

ST JULIAN'S PIER

LE POLLET

HIGH STREET

NORTH ESPLANADE

The Harbour

FOUNTAIN ST

VICTORIA RD

R. DU PRE

LE BORDAGE

VICTORIAN SHOP AND PARLOUR

SOUTH ESPLANADE

CASTLE PIER

CASTLE CORNET

HAUTEVILLE

HAUTEVILLE HOUSE (VICTOR HUGO'S HOME)

Havelet Bay

LA VALETTE

GEORGE RD

LES VARDES

LE VAL DES TERRES

LA VALETTE UNDERGROUND MILITARY MUSEUM

GUERNSEY AQUARIUM

N

0   100 m   250 m

0   600 ft

Duke of Normandie £ **⑤** Attractively renovated 18th-century hotel-pub with a good range of wines and bar lunches in a nostalgic maritime setting with oak beams, fires and courtyard barbecue.
🄰 Lefevre Street 🅃 01481 721431 🄲 Open daily for lunch and evening meals

La Frégate £££ **⑥** For a treat, book a table in this elegant hotel-restaurant at the top of the town. Panoramic views of the town and harbour and memorable French cuisine. 🄰 Les Cotils 🅃 01481 724624 🄲 Open daily for lunch and evening meals 🄸 Smart dress required

Moore's Patisserie £ **⑦** A civilized place for a shopping or sightseeing break. Luscious Austrian-style pastries or wholesome light lunches in smartly refurbished surroundings. On the same premises, try the cosy **Library Bar** for a drink or a carvery lunch.
🄰 Le Pollet 🅃 01481 724452 🄲 Open for lunch and early evening meals

Pelican's Café £ **⑧** Modern decor and friendly service in this clean coffee shop, which serves unpretentious fare with a touch of sophistication. 🄰 24 Le Pollet 🅃 01481 713636 🄲 Open Mon–Sat for breakfast, lunch and afternoon tea, closed Sun 🄸 No smoking, no credit cards

SHOPPING

St Peter Port's waterfront stores cater for visiting yachtsmen, while shops in the cobbled streets offer a VAT-free range of classy clothes, jewellery, cameras, electrical goods, perfumes and shoes. Children enjoy the National Trust's quaint **Victorian shop** 🄰 26 Cornet Street or **Guernsey Toys** 🄰 Victoria Road, for a genuine Guernsey teddy. In the old market behind the parish church flowers, seafood and local produce compete with foreign imports in the mornings; in summer on Thursday afternoons, stall holders don traditional costumes and the market place takes on a festive air, with candy-striped stalls and dancing in the evenings.

Northern Guernsey
island powerhouse

The northern tip of Guernsey is easily reached from Jersey. It is low-lying and peaceful, despite being quite densely populated (in parts at least). Much land lies under greenhouse glass or water catchment systems. Here, too, is Guernsey's only significant industrial centre, St Sampson. The cranes and warehouses of the island's main cargo port and the power station's fuming chimneys don't often feature on Guernsey's picture postcards, but if you enjoy ambling round a working port or looking at industrial archaeology you may appreciate St Sampson's gritty authenticity. It has some useful, reasonably priced shops too.

Several neolithic sites have been discovered in **Vale**, Guernsey's northernmost parish. Les Fouillages (small burial chambers) were unearthed on the golf course on **L'Ancresse Common** in 1978. Amateur archaeologists may like to track down the megalithic dolmens (passage graves) of La Varde and Dehus.

Tucked into a sheltered rock basin on the island's north-east tip is **Beaucette Marina**, full of classy-looking ocean-going yachts. If you enjoy walking or bird-watching, follow the coastal path on the headlands to see migrant birds in spring and autumn. The views are spectacular at any time of year. Castles and towers stud the headlands at every turn – **Vale Castel, Rousse Tower** and **Fort Doyle** are among the most impressive. Large stretches of sand and reefs lie exposed at low tide, especially in **L'Ancresse Bay** or around **Grand Havre**. L'Ancresse Common is a gorse-covered stretch of moor and pastureland dotted with pine trees and placid tethered cattle.

If you're an active sort, you might want to try the go-kart track just north of St Peter Port, or the windsurfing centres at **Cobo** and **L'Ancresse Bays**. Fishing and diving expeditions can be arranged too. All swimmers should be careful on these coasts – even the sheltered eastern side has deceptive currents.

THINGS TO SEE & DO
Guernsey Freesia Centre ★
For an insight into Guernsey's blooming mail-order flower business, visit these fragrant glasshouses to watch planting, picking and packing.
ⓐ Route Carré, St Sampson ⓣ 01481 248185 ⓛ Open 09.00–17.00
ⓘ Admission free

Oatlands Craft Centre ★★
This former brickworks houses a complex of craft studios and gift shops: glass blowing, pottery, silverwork and knitwear are just some of the things on show. Conservatory café. ⓐ Braye Road, St Sampson
ⓣ 01481 244282 ⓛ Open daily 09.30–17.00 ⓘ Admission free

⬢ *St Sampson's Harbour*

Saumarez Park & Folk Museum ★★★

Don't confuse this fine estate with St Martin's Sausmarez Manor, owned by a separate (and differently spelt!) branch of the ancient seigneurial family. Here, Guernsey's National Trust has set up a folk museum in the stable block, recreating typical period interiors, including a Victorian kitchen, parlour and washhouse. Nature trails, children's playground, tearooms and shop. ❸ Saumarez Park, Castel ❶ 01481 255384 ❺ Open 10.00–17.30 (Easter–Oct) ❶ Admission charge

Telephone Museum ★

A century of long-distance communications equipment, some still in working order, on display in a small suburban house. ❸ Cobo Road, Castel ❶ 01481 257904 ❺ Open Mon–Sat 10.00–17.00 (Apr–Sept) ❶ Admission free

RESTAURANTS & PUBS

Good daytime restaurants in northern Guernsey are thin on the ground, though it isn't difficult to get a snack. You may like to stock up with picnic provisions or fish and chips and find a quiet beach somewhere.

Cobo Bay Hotel ££ Ambitious combinations of sweet and savoury ingredients and lots of fresh fish are on the dinner menus in this agreeable seaside hotel. Ultra-attentive service and a good-value table d'hôte. ❸ Cobo Bay, Castel ❶ 01481 257102 ❺ Open daily

Fryer Tuck's Halfway Cafe £ More than a take-away chippie! Serves sit-down meals on the seafront, with salmon and steaks, at rock-bottom prices. ❸ 1 Commercial Place, St Sampson ❶ 01481 249448 ❺ Open Mon–Sat 06.30–14.15, Sun 09.00–14.15 ❶ Licensed, with parking

Hougue du Pommier ££ Non-residents welcome at this old pleasant farmhouse hotel near Cobo Bay. Filling lunch or evening bar snacks. Full à la carte in the restaurant ❸ La Route de la Hougue du Pommier, Castel ❶ 01481 256531 ❺ Open daily for lunch and evening meals

South-west Guernsey
cliffs and surf

South-west Guernsey has a strikingly varied shoreline. The west coast, scalloped into wide, low-lying bays of rock and sand, changes dramatically between high and low tide when the reefs lie exposed. With mighty Atlantic breakers, the coastline is popular with expert surfers, but novice swimmers should take care.

Round the dramatic **Pleinmont headland** on the southwest tip, the coast takes on a completely different character. Here the shoreline is cliff-fringed and rocky, hiding tiny, tidal scraps of sand and the waterline can be difficult and dangerous to reach along clifftop footpaths. Defensive structures line this daunting coast, from Martello towers to German gun emplacements. Most impressive is the gaunt tower in Pleinmont. Inland lie the parishes of **Torteval, St Pierre du Bois** and **St Saviour**, which are less developed than other parts of the island. Quiet farmland is interspersed with a web of tiny rural lanes where you can get thoroughly and enjoyably lost.

Be sure to drive carefully along the west coast road in rough weather when the tide is in. The waves sometimes wash alarmingly right over the sea walls – be prepared! In fine weather, though, the western seafront can be magical, especially at sunset when the rocks turn extraordinary hues of pink and gold. You can watch it from the fortified headlands, where parking places can be reached by quiet access tracks off the comparatively busy main road.

THINGS TO SEE & DO
Bruce Russell Gold & Silversmiths ★★★
Watch skilled craftsfolk hand-finishing an elegant range of jewellery and artefacts offered for sale in these 16th-century showrooms. Ancillary attractions include immaculate gardens and the **Furze Oven café**.
ⓐ Le Gron, St Saviour ☎ 01481 264321 ⏲ Open daily 09.00–17.00 (except Sun in winter) ⓘ Admission free

⬥ *Rocky cliffs fringe the south coast*

Cliff walks ★★★

Guernsey's hilly south coast is the prettiest part of the island for walking. Footpaths lead all the way along, past watch-towers, coves and headlands, free of traffic but accessible by lanes with parking places at various points. Take care: the cliffs may be unstable so don't stray from the marked paths.

Coach House Gallery ★★

Housed in sympathetically restored farm buildings, this light, airy gallery displays works by local artists, including crafts and original prints at a

wide range of prices. Visit the Framecraft art shop across the courtyard for artists' materials or a speedy framing service. ❷ Les Paysans Road, St Pierre du Bois ❶ 01481 265339 ◷ Open daily 11.00–17.00 all year ❶ Admission free

Fort Grey ★★

The stumpy white Martello tower on Rocquaine Bay contains a fascinating Shipwreck Museum, showing the perils of Guernsey's reef-strewn west coast. ❷ Rocquaine Coast Road, St Pierre du Bois ❶ 01481 265036 ◷ Open daily 10.00–17.00 (Apr–Oct) ❶ Admission charge

Lihou Island ★

The tiny, privately owned island of Lihou, off the L'Erée headland, makes an unusual walk at low tide. There is just one house and the remains of a Benedictine priory. Check tide tables carefully before you cross; the causeway is uncovered only for a few hours.

Strawberry Farm & Guernsey Woodcarvers ★★

Though under separate management, these attractions share facilities and can be seen on the same visit. The Strawberry Farm has turned its novel crop (over 50,000 strawberry plants in suspended growbags) into a tourist attraction, with gift and craft shops, play areas and tea gardens. The woodcarving studio produces a large range of attractive, portable souvenirs and furniture from over 60 types of timber. Watch skilled craftsmen turning, carving, French polishing, furniture-restoring and cabinet-making. ❷ Les Issues, St Saviour ❶ 01481 268015 ◷ Open daily 10.00–17.00 ❶ Admission free

Le Tricoteur ★

Watch the production process then check the prices of classic hand-finished Guernseys and other woollen and cotton goods in the shop. Children's and extra-large sizes are also available. ❷ Perelle Bay ❶ 01481 264040 ◷ Open Mon–Fri 08.30–17.00, Sat 08.30–16.00, closed Sun ❶ Admission free

RESTAURANTS & PUBS

This part of the island has a good range of eating places, including some of Guernsey's best. Most are easy to find along the larger roads, but you'll need a good navigator for the Café du Moulin.

Café du Moulin ££ Rapidly establishing a name as one of the island's foremost restaurants, this delightful old mill is huddled in one of the island's greenest valleys and adjoining a nature reserve. Teas and bar snacks and imaginative menus. Everything freshly prepared; vegetarian choices. Book ahead. No smoking in the dining room. ⓐ Rue de Quanteraine, St Pierre du Bois ⓣ 01481 265944 ⓛ Open daily (except Mon and Sun evening)

Fleur du Jardin ££ This charming farmhouse inn has an enviable reputation. Traditional bar food and more interesting restaurant fare with fresh fish and game. ⓐ King's Mills, Castel ⓣ 01481 257996 ⓛ Open daily for lunch and evening meals ⓘ Reservations recommended

Imperial Hotel ££ Three bars, a patio and garden, offer a choice of places to enjoy excellent cooking near a lovely stretch of coastline with cliff walks and beaches. ⓐ Pleinmont, Torteval ⓣ 01481 264044 ⓛ Open daily for snacks, lunch and evening meals with a huge carvery on Sun

Longfrie Inn £ Family-oriented country inn with plenty of satisfying but inexpensive bar food and cheerful menus for kids. Garden and play area. ⓐ Rue de Longfrie, St Pierre du Bois ⓣ 01481 263107 ⓛ Open daily for lunch and evening meals (except Mon and Sun evenings)

Taste of India ££ This traditional-looking cottage, known as Sunset Cottage, on the west coast offers an exotic Indian-inspired menu. No extra charge for enjoying the technicolour sunsets or a stroll along the strand! ⓐ L'Erée, St Pierre du Bois ⓣ 01481 264516 ⓛ Open daily from noon

South-east Guernsey
quiet lanes, secluded coves

The main roads close to St Peter Port are built up and congested with a surprising amount of rush-hour commuter traffic, but brief detours down the quiet lanes of St Martin lead to the idyllic, unspoilt headlands of Icart and Jerbourg, where secluded sandy coves nestle beneath dramatic cliffs. Icart is the highest headland on Guernsey.

More sheltered than the west coast or northern beaches, these coves are ideal for swimming, though some involve a steep trek. The best way to see this part of the island is on foot by following the waymarked coastal tracks. Alternatively, take a boat trip from St Peter Port harbour on a fine day and view the south coast from the sea.

Wherever you stay, Guernsey is small enough to allow you to choose your beach by wind direction and sun position. The beaches of south-east Guernsey are a good bet when westerly or northerly winds are blowing. They tend to be sunniest in the early part of the day.

THINGS TO SEE & DO
Catherine Best Studio ★
One of Guernsey's most renowned jewellery designers has a studio showroom in a converted windmill. Original handmade pieces using precious and semi-precious materials, in a wide range of traditional and modern designs. ❸ The Old Mill, Steam Mill Lanes, St Martin ❶ 01481 237771 ● Open Mon–Sat 09.00–17.30, Sun 09.30–17.00 ❶ Admission free

German Occupation Museum ★★
An authentic display of World War II memorabilia recounting the dark days of the German Occupation of Guernsey. The day-to-day trials of the islanders are brought vividly to life in crystal sets, diaries, press cuttings

◢ *Pleasant pursuits at Sausmarez Manor, St Martin*

and ration books. Tea rooms (sample some wartime parsnip coffee – if you dare). ❸ Near Forest parish church (opposite airport entrance turning) ❶ 01481 238205 ❶ Open Tues –Sun 10.00–17.00 (winter times vary) ❶ Admission charge

🔻 *Almost tropical, the beautiful Fermain Bay*

German Underground Hospital ★★

This dank, rambling tunnel complex, dug by slave labour, is one of the most chilling reminders of the German Occupation period on any of the Channel Islands. Despite the effort expended in its construction, it was scarcely used for medical purposes, and served mainly as an ammunition dump. ⓐ La Vassalerie Road, St Andrew ☎ 01481 239100 🕒 Open daily 10.00–noon and 14.00–16.00 (June), 10.00–noon and 14.00–16.30 (July–Aug) ; restricted hours in winter ❶ Admission charge

Guernsey Clockmakers & Little Chapel ★★

A collection of barometers and timepieces, from longcase clocks to novelty watches, many made on the premises. Nearby stands the photogenic Little Chapel, which claims to be the world's smallest church at only 5 m (5¹/₂ yds) long. Inspired by the grotto shrine at Lourdes, it is festooned with shells, pebbles and fragments of coloured china. ⓐ Les Vauxbelets, St Andrew ☎ 01481 236360 🕒 Open Mon–Fri 08.30–17.30, Sat 10.00–16.00 ❶ Admission free; chapel freely accessible all year; donations welcome

La Gran'mère du Chimquière ★

This ancient Bronze Age curiosity, whose name means 'the graveyard granny', stands by the gate of St Martin's parish church. The stone-carved female figure is believed to have magical powers and, even today, flower garlands and good-luck tokens are placed on her head, especially after wedding ceremonies. ⓐ St Martin's Church ❶ Admission free

Moulin Huet Pottery ★

A cottage workshop gallery hidden in a leafy lane leading to a pretty south-coast cove. The painter Renoir was inspired by this part of the island on a visit in 1882. Have a browse at the porcelain, stoneware, paintings and crafts on sale, or simply watch the pottery being made. ⓐ Moulin Huet, St Martin ☎ 01481 237201 🕒 Open Mon–Sat 09.00–16.00, Sun 10.00–noon (Easter to Christmas only) ❶ Admission free

Sausmarez Manor ★ ★ ★

This impressive stately home is occupied by one of the oldest and most distinguished families in the Channel Islands. Entertaining guided tours of the house highlight fine furnishings and ancestral anecdotes. Additional attractions include exotic woodland gardens, a miniature railway and a challenging pitch-and-putt course, plus a new sculpture trail. ⓐ Sausmarez Road, St Martin ⓣ 01481 235571 ⓛ House open Mon–Thurs 10.30 and 11.30 (Easter–Oct, plus afternoons June–Sept); other attractions 10.00–17.00 ⓘ Separate admission charges

RESTAURANTS & PUBS

Many of the most appealing restaurants in this part of the island are in beautifully located hotels. Full meals can be a bit pricey, but most places offer less formal bar snacks or teas too.

Bella Luce £**£** This long-established manor hotel in a rural setting is an island favourite. Bar meals and afternoon teas are served in the gardens on fine days, with traditional à la carte fare in the evenings. ⓐ Moulin Huet, St Martin ⓣ 01481 238764 ⓛ Open daily for lunch and evening meals

Le Chalet £**£** Nestling in woodland above Fermain Bay, this alpine-style restaurant has a sun terrace and bar for light refreshments, and a more lavish French restaurant. ⓐ Fermain Bay, St Martin (courtesy bus from St Peter Port except Sun) ⓣ 01481 235716 ⓛ Open daily for lunch and evening meals (Apr–Oct)

Idlerocks Hotel £**£** Following a devastating fire in 2003, the hotel stopped serving meals but its team plans to reopen the restaurant soon. A superb seaview setting overlooking Herm, Sark, Jersey and the French coastline in one of Guernsey's quietest spots makes a meal here a memorable occasion, so it is worth checking to see whether it has reopened in time for your visit. ⓐ Jerbourg Point, St Martin ⓣ 01481 237711 ⓦ www.idlerocks.com

Alderney
windswept delight

Alderney, the most northerly of the Channel Islands, lies just 14 km (8 miles) west of Normandy's Cotentin Peninsula. This 2½ km (1½ miles) wide and 5½ km (3½ miles) long island is the perfect place to unwind and offers something for almost everyone.

It does not take long to get to Alderney from Jersey, or indeed to discover the attraction of its unspoilt open landscapes, wonderful cliff walks and beautiful uncrowded beaches. Good leisure facilities and friendly pubs and restaurants add to the island's natural charms. At its heart lies the delightful town of St Anne, while Victorian fortresses stud the headlands.

Alderney was the first Channel Island to introduce duty-free goods. Alcohol and tobacco prices are worth checking wherever you see the sign. You may only buy if you are leaving the Bailiwick of Guernsey directly after your stay (e.g. for Jersey or the UK).

THINGS TO SEE & DO
Alderney Breakwater ★★

This huge, Victorian granite structure on the north-west coast of Alderney extends over half a mile into the sea. Its maintenance costs form Guernsey's contribution to the British Isles' defence budget.

Alderney Society Museum ★★

Housed in an old school, this small collection traces the island's history from prehistoric times. ⓐ Lower High St, St Anne ⓣ 01481 823222 ⓛ Open Mon–Fri 10.00–noon and 14.00–16.00; Sat and Sun 10.00–noon (Apr–Oct) ⓘ Admission charge

Alderney Railway ★★

The Channel Islands' last remaining railway, built to carry granite to the breakwater, offers 30-minute nostalgia rides in old London Underground carriages during the summer. Adults and children can also enjoy a ride in

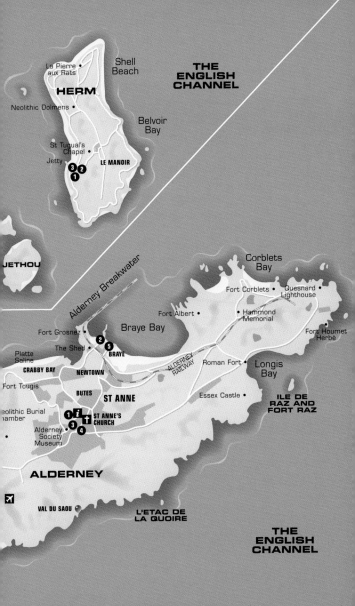

summer on the miniature railway in Mannez Quarry. ☎ 01481 822980 🕐 Open weekends and Bank Holidays in summer 14.00–16.45 ❶ Admission charge

🔺 *Quesnard Lighthouse*

Boat trips ★★

Trips on *Voyager* or *Lady Maris* survey Alderney's coastal scenery – alternatively hop to France or the other Channel Islands. The Alderney Tourist Information Centre in Victoria Street has information on trips. ☎ 01481 823737 ❶ Seasonal and weather dependant

Les Etacs Rocks ★★

Home to one of the British Isles' rare gannet colonies, birds sit beak to beak in a pungent top-dressing of guano. Nearby Burhou Island is home to a small group of puffins. Birdwatchers: don't forget your binoculars.

Fort Clonque ★

One of Alderney's Victorian forts, attractively restored by the Landmark Trust as holiday apartments, lies at the end of a concrete causeway (inaccessible at high tide). ⓐ Near Clonque beach

Hammond Memorial ★

Plaques in several languages commemorate the Russian, Polish and Jewish slave-workers who perished under German occupation while constructing Hitler's Atlantic Wall.

Quesnard Lighthouse ★

Dating from 1912, the Quesnard Lighthouse offers spectacular views of the razor-sharp reefs on this dangerous coast. Afternoon visits by arrangement with the tourist office. ⓐ Quesnard ☎ 01481 823737

St Anne's Church ★★

One of the finest Channel Island churches, built of Caen stone and restored after wartime damage. ❸ St Anne

Telegraph Tower ★

The high cliffs near this 19th-century signalling tower offer views of all the Channel Islands.

The Shed ★★

Items from a wrecked Elizabethan warship feature in this little museum. ❸ Braye Harbour ❶ 01481 823222 ❷ Open certain afternoons in summer; check with Alderney Society Museum ❶ Admission free

BEACHES

Alderney has some good stretches of sand on its northern shores, most of which are fairly easy to access. Some of the fastest tidal races in the world flow past the island. Cliffs make the southerly shore difficult to reach. The varied seabirds make Alderney's coastal walks interesting, but

⏶ *Fort Clonque, Alderney*

the many fortresses, some derelict, give it a forbidding air. **Braye Bay**, protected from westerly gales by the breakwater, is best for swimming and windsurfing. Quieter **Corblets Bay** is dominated by Fort Corblets and has safe bathing and good surf. **Longis Bay** – another sheltered stretch of sand on the eastern coast – is also popular.

RESTAURANTS & PUBS (see map on pages 80-81)

Alderney offers good eating and drinking places, nearly all clustered in St Anne or Braye Bay. Prices are slightly higher than the other islands due to freight costs, but licensing hours are more lenient; pubs stay open all day and every day, including Sunday. Seafood lovers should not miss the Seafood Festival in May.

Bumps Eating House ££ **1** Charming atmosphere with an impressive menu featuring international cuisine and an extensive wine list. ⓐ Braye St, St Anne ① 01481 823197

First and Last ££ **2** Primarily a seafood restaurant serving mouth-watering food that appeals to the eye and the taste buds. ⓐ Braye Harbour ① 01481 823162

Gannets £ **3** Attractive day-time café, licensed bistro and evening wine bar in a light, airy dining room decorated with soothing seascapes. Friendly service. Summer tables outside. ⓐ Victoria St, St Anne ① 01481 823098

Georgian House ££ **4** Civilized hotel-restaurant in an elegant period building. Specialities include seafood, barbecues and traditional Sunday roasts. Good-value lunchtime bar menus, but more expensive restaurant food only in evenings. ⓐ Victoria St, St Anne ① 01481 822471 ⓒ Open daily (except Tues evening) ⓘ Best to book

The Moorings £ **5** Offers good traditional bar meals, an à la carte menu with great seafood and al fresco dining around the

● *Braye Bay is ideal for swimming and offers a good choice of eateries*

barbecue in summer. Good value for money. ⓐ Braye Harbour
ⓣ 01481 822421 ⓒ Open daily

NIGHTLIFE

Only the larger islands offer any significant nightlife. Evening entertainment on the smaller islands is more likely to involve a jigsaw puzzle, a
game of Scrabble or a good book. Most hotels provide books and board
games for evenings and wet days, and impromptu events, such as quiz
nights or live music, may take place in local pubs. Evening entertainment
on Alderney mostly centres on its convivial pubs and restaurants. Visitors
are welcome to join in local island happenings – talks, slide shows, whist
drives, etc. You can generally find a game of dominoes, whist or bridge,
or a darts match, going on somewhere, and there's a tiny cinema in
Victoria Street.

Herm
jewel in the sand

Tiny Herm makes a marvellous outing for a fine day. With no cars or organized attractions, the island offers a simple but captivating mix of beautiful scenery, idyllic beaches and an irresistible invitation to unwind.

A mere 2.5 km (1½ miles) long and 1 km (½ mile) wide, you can walk round Herm in under two hours. Near the harbour is a Mediterranean- style 'village', colourwashed in ice-cream pastels and consisting of a hotel, pub and a handful of shops. Here you can have a drink, a snack or an excellent meal, and buy an imaginative range of souvenirs at good prices.

Central paths take you through woods and fields past the Tenant's castellated Manor and a tiny medieval chapel. Some outbuildings are converted into self-catering cottages, and the Seagull campground nestles discreetly among the trees. A pedigree herd of placid Guernsey cattle grazes in the surrounding farmland.

If you strike south, you climb along cliff paths overlooking rocks and reefs, and the privately owned island of Jethou (inaccessible to visitors). The low-lying northern routes lead over heathland fringed by glorious belts of sand. Wildlife flourishes on Herm with its hosts of seabirds, butterflies and riotous flowers. Yet every artificial feature, from farm gates and fences to beach cafés and holiday cottages, is kept in tip-top order.

 The early morning 'milk boat' ferry offers a reduced day return to Herm – and a longer stay on the island. Remember to listen to the weather forecast, as you'll be out of doors for much of the time.

ISLAND RULES
Herm has a few 'house rules' designed to maintain its peaceful attractions. Visitors are requested to keep pets under control, and not to pick plants, leave litter or play transistor radios in public.

THINGS TO SEE & DO

Le Manoir ★★

Herm's real 'village' centres around the imposing 15th-century manor, now the residence of the Wood family. The medieval-looking 'keep' is only a century old. Near the manor house are the island's power station, workshops and unobtrusive modern farm buildings.

Neolithic dolmens ★

In ancient times, Herm was considered a sacred place and served as a burial ground. Traces of several stone tombs remain towards the north of the island.

La Pierre aux Rats ★

A large, prehistoric standing stone served as a seamark for centuries until quarrymen removed it in the 19th century, thinking it was just another useful lump of granite. Local sailors protested and the present obelisk was put in its place.

St Tugual's Chapel ★★

This quaint little building dates from the 11th century. The unusual belltower is its most striking feature. It contains attractive stained glass, and a memorial to the Tenant's wife. Informal services are held every Sunday.

○ *Belvoir Bay with Shell Beach beyond*

BEACHES

Herm's pride and joy is **Shell Beach**, on the north-east shore. This is a magnificent stretch of sparkling quartz and shell fragments which looks truly tropical on a fine day and is the perfect place for beachcombing, sunbathing and sandcastles. Rock pools trap fascinating pockets of sealife at low tide, and the clear, gently shelving water is ideal for snorkelling. As its name suggests, the sand consists of millions of sparkling shells, some carried from the tropics on the Gulf Stream.

Herm's northern coast is an almost continuous belt of sand and dunes at low tide, easily reached if you're prepared to walk. Near the harbour the shoreline is muddier and rockier, and good for trying your luck with a shrimping net. **Belvoir Bay** is a more intimate sandy cove further south (beware of strong currents at low tide) with a café and toilets.

RESTAURANTS & PUBS (see map on pages 80-81)

Some summer ferry tickets include lunch or dinner, but Herm operates seasonally, and in the winter the island's pubs and cafés may be closed. Check before you sail. There are no grocery shops, but you can always take a picnic. Herm's oysters are famed throughout the Channel Islands.

The Mermaid Tavern £ ❶ The 'village inn' offers good snacks, full lunches and evening meals for most of the year. Barbecues and outside tables in summer; roaring fires in chilly weather. ❶ 01481 710170 ◷ Open daily (summer); Tues, Wed, Fri and Sat (winter)

The Ship Inn ££ ❷ This pleasant pub-restaurant is part of the White House hotel (see below), offering lunchtime fare and more elaborate evening meals at the Captain's Table (inclusive ferry/dinner packages available). ❶ 01481 722159 ◷ Open daily (Apr–Oct)

The White House £££ ❸ Herm's only hotel is primarily for resident guests but, space permitting, day visitors may book ahead for dinner only. ⓐ Near the harbour ◷ Open daily (Apr–Oct) ❶ 01481 722159 ❶ Smart dress, no smoking in the dining room

HERM'S TENANT

In 1949, Major Peter Wood and his wife Jenny took over a long lease on the island from the States of Guernsey. Their enthusiastic enterprise and hard work has resulted in today's civilized miniature paradise. Financed by dairy farming and tourism, Herm continues to be managed by members of the Wood family (the Major died in 1998 and his wife in 1991). The resident population of 50 is doubled in summer by seasonal staff. Local children are educated in the tiny island school. Herm also generates its own electricity and has its own water supply and drainage systems. Morning boats transport about 900 litres (over 200 gallons) of creamy milk daily to Guernsey for processing, and offload the empty churns with Herm-bound passengers in the afternoon.

NIGHTLIFE

If sea air, good food and exercise don't suggest an early night, you may find yourself practising the age-old, but much-neglected art of conversation. To encourage social interaction, television is deliberately banished at Herm's White House Hotel.

🔺 Herm's beautiful Shell Beach

Sark
feudal showcase

Less than 10 km (6 miles) east of Guernsey lies a quaint political fossil – a last vestige of European feudalism. Less than 5 sq km (2 sq miles), Sark is home to about 550 permanent residents, but welcomes over a hundred times as many visitors every year. Five hours or so between ferry rides is short shrift to give this pretty place. Stay longer if you can – especially in spring, when Sark is carpeted with flowers.

Sark is a jagged rock plateau perching on 90 m (300 ft) high cliffs, gashed by deep valleys leading to the sea. It is almost two islands, for the smaller, southerly island, called **Little Sark**, is only attached to its big sister by a knife-edge ridge called **La Coupée**. Sark's scenery and individuality attract enough daytrippers to cause bicycle jams in high season. But if you stray off the beaten tyre-tracks, you will find secret coves and crevices all to yourself.

Like its close neighbour, Herm, Sark allows no visiting motor vehicles, and access to the island is by ferry only (helicopters may land in dire emergencies). A tractor-bus service saves ferry passengers the climb up and down **Harbour Hill.** At the top of the hill lies the village of Toytown proportions.

The island's famous Dame, Sibil Hathaway, remembered for her courage during the German occupation, has been succeeded as Seigneur of Sark by her grandson, whose residence, **La Seigneurie**, is Sark's most impressive building. The Seigneur still holds a few privileges first granted by Elizabeth I in 1565. He is the only Sark-dweller permitted to keep doves, for example, or an unspayed bitch. More lucratively, he is entitled to receive one-thirteenth (Le Trezième) of the value of any Sark property that changes hands.

You can get to Sark from St Helier, Jersey, in around 50 minutes by ferry

---

THINGS TO SEE & DO
Boat trips ★
If you're only on Sark for a day, a boat trip is a bit ambitious, but in calm weather it's an enjoyable way to see the island's intricate, cave-pocked cliffs and study the seabirds. **Sark Tourist Information Centre** has more information. ⓐ On Harbour Hill ⓣ 01481 832345

Carriage rides ★
See Sark the leisurely way – by horse power. Patient carthorses await the ferry boats in summer. You can pre-book a jaunt from Guernsey, or negotiate the fare on arrival for one- or two-hour excursions. ⓣ 01481 832345

⬤ *Beneath La Coupée lies Grand Grève Bay*

La Coupée ★★

This breathtaking neck of rock, linking Little Sark to the main island, was fenced by prisoners-of-war, and is just wide enough for a tractor or a horse-drawn carriage to pass across, with dizzying drops to either side.

Le Creux Harbour ★

Tunnels lead to this pretty, rock-walled harbour from the more modern and practical landing stage at La Maseline.

Prison ★

Sark's curious little jail stands in the village. It has just two cells, and is still occasionally used before dispatching miscreants to Guernsey for trial.

⬥ *Horse-drawn carriages are the main transport on Sark*

Sark Occupation Museum ★★

This museum conveys aspects of island life under the jackboot during World War II; luckily Sark escaped fairly lightly, with no serious food shortages and no fortifications. Items on display include photographs of the redoubtable Dame of Sark dealing with her uninvited guests.
☎ 01481 832345 🕐 Open Easter–Sept ❶ Admission charge

La Seigneurie ★★

You can't look round the Seigneur's granite manor house, but his varied, beautiful gardens are well worth seeing, with their roses, tender plants, a hedge maze and a Victorian greenhouse. Look out for the strange Gothic *colombier* (dovecot) and the antique cannon. ☎ 01481 832345
🕐 Open Mon–Fri 10.00–17.00 (Easter–Oct, plus Sat and Sun in high summer) ❶ Admission charge

Silver mines ★

The shafts and ventilation chimneys of Sark's 19th-century mining days can still be seen on Little Sark. The mines were never profitable, and were abandoned after a tragedy in 1845.

BEACHES

Access to most of Sark's cliff-backed coves involves a steep climb. Easiest to reach (from Dixcart Hotel) is **Dixcart Bay** – safe, sandy and scenic, spanned by an arch of natural rock. Neighbouring **Derrible Bay** has sand only at low tide. Adventurous explorers may discover **Pot Bay** or the deep tidal pool on Little Sark that is **Venus Pool**.

RESTAURANTS & PUBS (see map on page 80-81)

Sark's most sophisticated eating places are its hotel-restaurants, several of which vie for placings in good food guides. If all you want is a drink or a snack, no problem, however, choice is restricted in winter, when most hotels close. Buy picnic provisions and cakes at the village's Island Stores.

Aval du Creux Hotel ££ ❶ An easy place to find, with simple lunches, cream teas, and dinner in a pleasant setting, as well as outside tables. ❷ Next to the tourist office on Harbour Hill ❸ 01481 832036 ⏰ Open daily 11.00–17.30 (Apr–Oct)

Bel Air Inn £ ❷ This inn offers a good choice of dishes with the emphasis on seafood, steaks and pasta. Contemporary feel. Two bars with traditional cuisine. ❷ Harbour Hill ❸ 01481 832053 ⏰ Open daily

Dixcart Bay Hotel ££ ❸ One of Sark's oldest and most respected hotels (pronounced 'dee-cart') welcomes non-residents with a tasty range of snacks and full meals. Children's menus and seafood specialities. ❸ 01481 832015 ⏰ Open all year

Hotel Petit Champ ££ ❹ A west-coast setting with sea views accompanies everything from sandwiches to candlelit dinners. Lobster and crab. Sheltered garden. ❸ 01481 832046 ⏰ Open Easter–Oct

AN ISLAND OF YOUR OWN

'So, you like my island, Mr Bond ...' A separate island, **Brecqhou**, lies a stone's throw off Sark's northern tip. This was privately purchased in 1993 by the wealthy Barclay brothers – twin businessmen whose reclusive entrepreneurial activities cause much local gossip. Passing ferries give a tantalizing glimpse of a huge, newly built Gothic castle rising from Brecqhou. This extraordinary lair was constructed by a Guernsey workforce sworn to secrecy. Rumours of nuclear bunkers, summit conferences and private casinos flourish, fuelled by vigorous denials, and determined resistance to trespassing.

◔ View of the intriguing, privately owned Brecqhou island

🍴 **La Sablonnerie Hotel** ££ ❺ A charming garden setting on Little Sark is just one of the attractions of this acclaimed farmhouse hotel. Others include fresh fish and home-grown produce, Sark cream teas and seafood platters. ☎ 01481 832061 🕐 Open Easter–Oct

🍴 **Stocks Island Hotel** ££ ❻ The Courtyard Bistro offers a good range of snacks, teas, light and full meals, with more elaborate dining in the Cider Press Restaurant. Chinese and Indian evenings. Children's menus and tables outside. ☎ 01481 832001 🕐 Open 10.00–22.00 (Apr–Oct)

NIGHTLIFE

Sark's social scene revolves round the Island Hall in the village centre, where there is table tennis, badminton and a billiard table. In summer, just occasionally, concerts and recitals are held.

SHORT TRIPS
French towns and coastline

Apart from excursions to the other Channel islands, it's an easy hop from Jersey to France. St Malo, with its ramparts, cobbled streets, craft shops and fish restaurants, makes a delightful day out and there is a daily direct ferry service operating from St Helier (journey time is 1 hour 15 minutes). If you take a car across, from St Malo, it's possible to reach the elegant seaside resort of Dinard on the opposite side of the river Rance (visit the amazing Tidal Barrage on the way). Upstream is the gorgeous medieval town of Dinan and, 45 minutes by car to the east, the magical abbey fortress of Mont St Michel rises like a mirage from the bay. Don't forget to take your passport!

Food & drink

EATING OUT

Unlike the unfortunate islanders who endured wartime occupation on grisly fare like parsnip coffee and peapod tea, today's holidaymakers in Jersey can expect good rations. Eating is an important part of Jersey life. Local ingredients, especially seafood, market garden vegetables, and dairy produce, are renowned for their freshness and quality. But many staples have to be imported, so the cost of eating out, or shopping for self-catering, may be higher than you expect.

The Tourist Information Centre's 'Eating Out' guides give useful restaurant suggestions, though they do not always list the more exclusive eating places. If you prefer to eat and drink without a garnish of cigarette ash, pick up the 'smoke-free' guide to Channel Island pubs and restaurants.

BUDGET EATING

Excellent, imaginative cooking is still on offer at moderate prices. Many tourist restaurants stay heartily traditional. Whatever the map suggests, culinary styles are closer to England than to France. Croissants and baguettes are on sale in the bakeries, but you are more likely to find a classic British fry-up on your hotel breakfast plate. Traditional carvery roasts are always popular at Sunday lunchtimes.

Dozens of friendly, family-oriented pubs offer well-tried favourites like ploughman's lunches and chilli con carne, though these are not the only things on bar menus. There is no shortage of cafés for cream teas, fish and chip shops for filling take-aways, and Indian, Chinese or Italian restaurants to provide reliable, inexpensive solutions to hunger pangs.

SEAFOOD

Finned or shelled, fish dishes feature on nearly every island menu. In the fast, tidal waters surrounding the Channel Islands, pollution levels are much lower than in some holiday destinations, so eating shellfish is less

● *Succulent Jersey crab for sale*

like playing Russian roulette with your stomach. Besides crab, brill and sea-bass, look out for Sark lobster and Herm oysters.

In the Channel Islands, humble British fish and chips attain classic status, but you will also find more elaborate French-style dishes like those popular in nearby Brittany and Normandy. Conger eel soup is a local favourite. Some expensive seafoods, such as spider crab, are sold by weight rather than by portion. Check carefully when you order to avoid a nasty shock when you receive the bill.

FRUIT & VEGETABLES

The first glasshouses on the islands were built to grow grapes in 1795; today, huge acreages of Jersey and Guernsey are under glass, although crops have altered in line with commercial pressures. Tomatoes, ousted by subsidized imports, have often given way to flowers. Market gardening is still important, however. Jersey Royal new potatoes, boiled and buttered with herbs, are a dish fit for a queen or king.

⬥ *Enjoying lunch in the sun*

Strawberries, celery, courgettes and many salad crops are raised for local consumption as well as the export trade. You'll often see produce on sale in little hatches by the roadsides, with an honesty box for the money.

DAIRY PRODUCE

Most people know about Channel Island 'gold top' milk with its high butterfat content. Butter and cream are produced in huge quantities, enriching local menus everywhere. Apart from a little Guernsey cheddar, you won't see much island-produced cheese – the milk sours too quickly.

CAKES

All kinds of cakes and scones appear in tea and coffee shops. Local choices include Jersey Wonders (a kind of doughnut), *fiottes* (balls of sweet pastry) or Guernsey *gâche* (pronounced 'gosh') – a fruit tea bread. You can some-times buy this ready buttered by the slice – good for a picnic! Don't forget to try some Channel Island fudge – available in an amazing range of flavours.

TRADITIONAL DISHES

One recipe widely promoted as an island classic is known as a bean crock, or bean jar – a rib-sticking casserole of pork, beans and onions. You may also come across black butter, which, despite its name, contains no dairy products at all. It's a long-brewed mixture of apples, sugar, lemons and cider, flavoured with liquorice. Try it spread on a slice of *gâche*.

DRINKS

The Normans introduced cider to the islands, but today beer is more popular. The Channel Islands also produce their own version of a cream liqueur, rather like Baileys. You may find an apple brandy on Jersey, made at La Mare Vineyards. Local beers you'll see everywhere include Mary Ann (Jersey) and Guernsey Brewery ales. Randalls no longer brews its own beer, but imports real ale and owns many Channel Island pubs.

THE ORMER

The mysterious ormer, a large mollusc like an asymmetrical limpet, derives its name from the French 'oreille de mer' (sea ear) – the Channel Islands being the northern limit of its habitat.

Unfortunately this local delicacy is now rare due to over-fishing. As such, strict regulations apply to the collection of ormers. They must only be harvested between the months of September and April, and only on the first day of the full moon and for the three days after. During this period, Jersey men and women scour the rocks to find the sought-after ormer. These rules are strictly policed and heavy fines are levied on offenders.

Once found, the ormer is prised from the underside of rocks by hand and carried to shore in a traditional ormer basket. It is then beaten, cooked in the oven as a casserole or served with gravy, carrots and onions. The ormer's striking mother-of-pearl inner shell is also used as decoration on houses and is used in jewellery.

Shopping

The Channel Islands market themselves as an inexpensive destination because duties are low and there is no VAT. Freight costs can erode this advantage and you should take advice before arranging for purchases to be shipped directly to the UK – you may end up having to pay VAT when they pass through customs. Also, do not forget that non-EU customs restrictions apply to any luxury purchased in the Channel Islands that you take back to the UK. Alcohol and tobacco are cheap, but savings on other goods are not always as great as you might expect. Prices vary significantly from one outlet to another, and from island to island, so shop around.

Look out for the 'Genuine Jersey' logo, indicating that the product is, as its name implies, genuinely made or produced on the island. This means that visitors, as well as residents, can ensure they are buying real, local

◆ Browsing for antiques in the side streets of St Helier

products. Dairy produce, honey, pottery, oysters, wines, beers, locally made jewellery, needlework, wooden artefacts and artworks are among the products that currently display this distinctive red logo.

ST HELIER

St Helier has the best shopping centres and streets in Jersey, but there are good (and sometimes cheaper) shops elsewhere on the island, such as at the Quennevais Shopping Centre in St Brelade. The markets and some shops are closed on Thursday afternoons, although many stay open into the evening in the height of the summer. There is no general Sunday trading in Jersey. In St Helier, head for the area around King Street and Queen Street – a good starting point for a shopping spree.

PERFUME & COSMETICS

St Helier is full of perfumeries, offering expensive, big-name brands, with everything from Estée Lauder to Chanel. There are a few smaller, chemist-style outlets that offer less expensive options as well.

FLOWERS & BULBS

Send a bouquet of freesias or roses to someone at home – all you have to do is fill in an address form and pay up. The biggest mail-order firm is Jersey's Flying Flowers, but most florists will advise you on which flowers to choose and how best to have them delivered home. Lower-key operations include the Sunset Nursery (St Peter) and Haute Tombette (St Mary) in Jersey. There is also a good garden centre attached to Longueville Manor, St Clement.

PHILATELY, ANTIQUES & BOOKS

To buy commemorative issues, visit the main post offices in St Helier, where large displays of stamps can be seen. The main one is in Broad Street, although there is a network throughout the island. Bygone-hunters will find numerous specialist shops dotted around in the side streets of St Helier. For books, try Bodhi Tree Book Shop in St Brelade or The Printed Word Bookshop in St Helier.

ISLAND CRAFTS

For one-stop centres where you can do all your souvenir buying in one go, head for the Craft and Shopping Village attached to Jersey's Living Legend attraction (see page 45) or, when you're visiting Guernsey, head for the Oatlands Craft Centre in St Sampson.

JEWELLERY

Some of Jersey's largest jewellery showrooms are Jersey Goldsmiths at Lion Park, St Lawrence, and Jersey Pearl in North End Five Mile Road, St Ouen. Compare prices with retailers in St Helier. Note that Channel Island gold and silver is not subject to the same rigorous assay and hallmarking process as it is in the UK. Any 'guarantee' offered with jewellery generally refers to the quality of workmanship, rather than any intrinsic value.

KNITWEAR

A genuine Channel Island sweater makes an excellent souvenir purchase. Jerseys come in many shapes, colours and styles, but a classic Guernsey sweater is instantly recognisable. Admiral Nelson spotted the potential of this warm, hardwearing fisherman's garment and recommended it for the British navy. The oiled wool is specially stitched, twisted and seamed to repel water. The practical design is stylish too, worn by men or women. Traditional, hand-finished Guernseys are produced at the Jersey Woollen Mills at St Ouen. For a sweater with a difference, try an Alderney, sold at Alderney's Channel Jumper shop near Braye Harbour on the island.

▶ The pedestrianized area of St Helier offers some great shopping

Kids

Jersey welcomes kids and there's plenty for them to do, although remember that the island has a leisurely way of life. Rushing about is not in the usual vocabulary, so be aware that children won't necessarily find lively attractions, such as theme parks, throughout the whole of the island. They will find plenty of sporting activities though, such as swimming, go-karting, horse riding and tennis, and fun holiday pursuits like beachcombing.

TOP ACTIVITIES

The high-tech **Living Legend** complex (see page 45) is one of Jersey's best all-round family attractions – an entertaining way to absorb a bit of island history.

The best museums for children are those run by the Jersey Museums Service, including: **Elizabeth Castle**, which offers battlement climbs and a ride on an amphibious 'duck truck' (see page 20); **Mont Orgueil**, Gorey's medieval castle (see page 17); St Helier's excellent **Maritime Museum**, with lots of hands-on seafaring (see page 23); and the **Hamptonne Country Life Museum**, with its costumed interpreters and farm animals (see page 49). There's also plenty to see at the **Jersey Museum** (see page 23) and **La Hougue Bie** (see page 26). Catch a ride in the vintage Museum Services Heritage Bus if you're visiting the out-of-town sights.

Samarès Manor's falconry displays and farm animals will entertain children, along with wooden toys and cream teas (see page 27). On a wet day, the **Fort Regent complex** offers stacks of ideas to burn off energy

JERSEY ZOO

Entertaining and educational, Jersey Zoo's friendly style ensures few children escape without forming a meaningful relationship with a gorilla or a flat-tailed tortoise. There is an audiovisual show and there are lots of fascinating special displays on endangered species, breeding programmes or releases into the wild.

(see page 22). See what over three million pearl shells look like at the **Shell Garden** in St Aubin. Mollusc shells have been embedded in cement to create shell churches, mermaids, boats and more. ☎ 01534 743561

BEACHCOMBING

Remember those childhood seaside holidays full of rock pools and sandcastles? Jersey's beaches are the perfect place to relive those simple, old-fashioned pleasures. Armed with buckets, spades and shrimping nets, children can have days of cost-free fun. Tidal seawater pools also offer sheltered bathing for older children. But remember that the red flag means dangerous conditions and no swimming; yellow means only good swimmers should take to the water; and a green flag indicates that conditions are safe.

EXCURSIONS

Jersey offers island-hopping excursions to Guernsey, Herm, Sark and Alderney. Even France seems a mere stone's throw away. Channel Island waters can be very choppy, so choose a calm day. If you're planning a visit to Alderney, a trip in one of Aurigny's tiny canary-coloured Trislander planes is a real adventure for kids. Look out for *Joey*, the star of the fleet with a red nose and big eyes.

🔺 *Passing time on the beach*

Festivals & events

Jersey loves festivals, carnivals and special events and is host to many throughout the year. Some of the biggest annual events on the island are listed below, though you'll find many other things going on. Precise dates vary from year to year, so check with the tourist office. Most are geared to the main holiday season (Easter to October). Besides the normal public holidays observed in the UK, the Channel Islands commemorate Liberation Day (9 May – the end of German occupation), and Remembrance Sunday (mid-November) with fervour.

The colourful parade of the **Battle of Flowers**, with flower-dressed floats, is irresistible if you're on Jersey in mid-August, while St Aubin has a **food fair** in July and there's an **international air display** in September. In August, the island goes 'Wet & Wild' with a week-long **Water Festival**, including wakeboarding, sailing, surfing and scuba diving opportunities. Other festivities on Jersey include:

- **Jazz Festival** (April/May) International stars in a week-long festival
- **Good Food Festival** (May/June) Wine-tastings and traditional dishes
- **Alderney Seafood Festival** (May) Not to be missed
- **Early Summer Festival** (June) Horticultural displays
- **Floral Festival** (July) A week of horticultural themes
- **World Music Festival** (September) A week of music around the globe
- **Food Festival** (October) A celebration of Jersey's food, with around 40 restaurants taking part
- **La Fête de Noué** (December) Christmas festival

OTHER ISLAND EVENTS

Guernsey has its share of festivals and carnivals, and on Alderney there's an **autumn juggling festival**. The island also hosts its **Alderney Week** in August with fancy dress parades, children's races and tug-of-war contests, with bonfires and fireworks to follow.

▶ *The colourful Battle of Flowers procession*

Sports & activities

Jersey offers a wide range of organized sports facilities. Jersey's Fort Regent (see page 22) in St Helier is a large complex that provides one-stop fitness in the form of swimming pools, tennis and squash courts. The island also has the indoor Les Quennevais Sports Centre (see page 47) in St Brelade, and an outdoor sports complex at the Jersey Recreation Grounds in St Clement.

WATER SPORTS

With all that sea on the doorstep, it's hardly surprising that there's plenty for waterbabies to do. Windsurfing enthusiasts should head for St Brelade's Bay or Grouville Bay for tuition or equipment. Waterskiing is available at the Jersey Seasports Centre in St Aubin. Diving is an attractive proposition in the clear waters around the Channel Islands, but you should take advice about currents. Wreck diving is a speciality, and there are diving centres in St Helier and Bouley Bay (trial dives are offered).

For novices, surfing here should probably remain a spectator sport, but experienced surfers may like to pit their skill against the Atlantic breakers of Jersey's St Ouen's Bay. Other watery activities include canoeing, rowing, pedalos, jet-skiing, parascending, speedboating and 'banana boats' – available from the main water sports centres at St Aubin, Gorey or St Brelade.

SAILING

The ritzy marinas around the Channel Islands soon tell you these waters represent nirvana for many yachtsfolk. If you're not lucky enough to own some ocean-going gin palace, you can always hire one, skippered or bareboat. Jersey is a good choice for novice sailors, although you can sail the waters around the other islands too.

FISHING

Channel Island waters attract a wide range of species. Sea and wreck-fishing boats can be chartered on most of the islands.

⬤ *Riding the surf, St Brelade's Bay*

GOLF

The enthusiasm for harrying small white balls into tiny holes knows no bounds on the Channel Islands. So many courses have sprung up that it's surprising they don't overlap. Egged on by resident golfing millionaires, Jersey now has half a dozen greens, not counting numerous pitch-and-putts and mini-golf courses. Two of these, the Royal Jersey at Grouville and La Moye near St Ouen's Bay, are prestigious clubs that accept only handicapped players from other recognized clubs. Less socially daunting courses are available at Les Ormes, Wheatlands, Les Mielles and Jersey Recreation Grounds. Book ahead (weekdays are cheaper) and check equipment hire.

HORSE RIDING

Many schools offer tuition and escorted hacking. Jersey has over half a dozen stables, and a spectacularly set race course at Les Landes, where British and French horses compete. Tourist offices can supply lists of riding schools and racing fixtures.

RACQUET SPORTS

Tennis, squash and badminton courts can be hired at the main sports complexes.

MOTOR SPORTS

Sand-racing, hillclimbing, rallies and motocross events are organized at various times throughout the year on Jersey. The Tourist Information Office in Liberation Square, St Helier, is the best place to find out what's happening. ☎ 01543 500888

BOWLS

Lawn bowls can be played in several locations on Jersey, including the Jersey Recreation Grounds. Some places have a strict dress code. If you are nipping over to Guernsey you can play outdoor bowls at Beau Séjour, indoors at Hougue du Pommier and Fort Regent. Ten-pin bowling is available at the well-equipped Jersey Bowl complex near the airport.

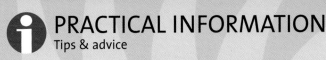

Preparing to go

GETTING THERE

By far the best way to visit Jersey is as part of an inclusive package, although travelling independently by booking a flight and accommodation is popular too. Jersey is well served by airlines, and there are both regular scheduled and charter flights from around 30 airports in the UK, including Aberdeen, Birmingham, the London airports, Manchester, Leeds, Liverpool and Norwich. Travelling by sea to Jersey is easy from Poole, Portsmouth and Weymouth. For information on tour operators featuring Jersey, visit Ⓦ www.abta.com.

BEFORE YOU LEAVE

Holidays should be about fun and relaxation, so avoid last-minute panics and stress by making your preparations well in advance. You do not need inoculations to travel to Jersey, but it is worth checking that you and your family are up-to-date with the basics, such as tetanus. If you take prescription medicines, make sure you have enough to last the whole trip. Consider packing a small first-aid kit containing plasters, antiseptic cream, travel sickness pills, insect repellent and/or bite-relief cream, upset stomach remedies and painkillers. Take plenty of sunscreen as Jersey can get very hot in the summer. Don't be deceived by a cool breeze and, for children in particular, choose a high factor lotion. Remember, too, to make arrangements for the care of your pets while you are away – book them into a reputable cat or dog hotel, or make arrangements with a trustworthy neighbour to ensure that they are properly fed, watered and exercised in your absence.

DOCUMENTS

The most important documents you will need are your tickets and passport, plus your driving licence if you are planning to take your car or hire one while on Jersey. If you plan to have more than one driver of the vehicle make sure that they, too, have their driving licence. Although passports are not needed to travel to the Channel Islands, you will want them if you are thinking of an excursion to France. Remember photo ID will be required by your airline and if you need medical assistance. Make sure that your passports are up-to-date and have at least three months left to run (to be safe, six months is even better). All children, including newborn babies, need their own passport now. It generally takes at least three weeks to process a passport renewal. This can be longer in the run-up to the summer months. Contact the **Passport Agency** for the latest information on how to renew your passport and the processing times involved. ☎ 0870 521 0410 Ⓦ www.ukpa.gov.uk.

Always check the details on your travel tickets well before your departure, ensuring that the timings and dates are correct.

MONEY

Although Jersey have their own notes and coins, UK currency is legal tender in the Channel Islands so you do not need to worry about currency exchange or travellers' cheques. However, you should make sure that your credit, charge and debit cards are up to date – you do not want them to expire mid-holiday – and that your credit limit is sufficient to allow you to make those holiday purchases. Also, don't forget to check your PIN numbers in case you haven't used them for a while – your bank or card company will assist you. Do not draw out too much money from cash-points, as Channel Islands currency will not be accepted back in the UK.

INSURANCE

Have you got adequate cover for your holiday? Check that your policy covers you adequately for loss of possessions and valuables, for activities you might want to try – such as scuba diving, horse-riding, or water-sports – and for emergency medical and dental treatment, including flights home if required. You do not need a EHIC medical card (which replaced the E111) but you do need proof of UK citizenships to obtain treatment. For further information, call EHIC enquiries line (☎ 0845 605 0707) or visit the Department of Health website (Ⓦ www.dh.gov.uk).

CLIMATE

As one of the most southerly of the Channel Islands, Jersey has one of the best sunshine records in the British Isles. It enjoys long, hot summer days with around 2,000 hours of sunshine a year, and mild winters. Despite a deceptive sea breeze, the air is clear and the ultra-violet rays are strong. Don't forget to slap on the sun-cream.

SECURITY

Take sensible precautions while you are away:

- Cancel milk, newspapers and other regular deliveries so that post and milk do not pile up on the doorstep.
- Let the postman know where to leave bulky mail (ideally with a next-door neighbour) that will not go through your letterbox.
- If possible, arrange for a friend or neighbour to visit regularly to close and open your curtains, and switch the lights on and off. Or buy electrical timing devices that will switch lights and radios on and off.
- Let Neighbourhood Watch representatives know that you will be away so that they can keep an eye on your home.
- If you have a burglar alarm, make sure that it is working properly and is switched on when you leave (you may find that your insurance policy requires this). Ensure that a neighbour is able to gain access to the alarm to turn it off, just in case it is set off accidentally.
- If you are leaving cars unattended, put them in a garage, if possible, and leave a key with a neighbour in case the alarm goes off.

AIRPORT PARKING & ACCOMMODATION

If you intend to park your car while you are away, or stay the night at an airport hotel before or after your flight, you should book well ahead to take advantage of discounts or cheap off-airport parking. Airport accommodation gets booked up several weeks in advance, especially during the height of the holiday season. Check whether the hotel you are staying in offers free parking for the duration of the holiday – often the savings made on parking costs can make the accommodation price significantly more attractive.

BAGGAGE ALLOWANCE & PACKING TIPS

Baggage allowances vary according to the airline, destination and the class of travel, but 20 kg (44 lb) per person is the norm for luggage that is carried in the hold (it usually tells you what the weight limit is on your ticket); in addition you are allowed one item of cabin baggage weighing no more than 5 kg (11 lb), and measuring 46 by 30 by 23 cm (18 by 12 by 9 inches). You can carry your duty-free purchases, umbrella, handbag, coat, camera, etc as hand baggage. Large items – surfboards, golf-clubs, collapsible wheelchairs and pushchairs – are usually charged as extras and it is a good idea to let the airline know in advance that you want to bring these.

For your trip to Jersey, you should consider packing the following:

- Photo ID and/or Passport – the latter is necessary if you think you may be tempted by the idea of hopping over to France for the day.
- Checklist of UK prices for items you may want to buy while you are on holiday. Because of low taxation and the absence of VAT, cameras, electronic goods, clothing, perfumes, cigarettes, alcohol and jewellery are all cheaper than in other parts of Europe – but not always: some retailers mark their prices up to take account of the cost of freighting the goods to the Channel Islands. Do your homework beforehand.
- Camera.
- Driving licence – you will need this to hire a car (even if you've prebooked one) or a moped. Photocopies of your licence are not accepted on the islands.
- Wet weather gear – sadly, sunshine cannot be guaranteed.
- Sensible footwear – you're bound to want to do some walking at some point, if only round St Helier's shops.
- Warm sweater – but save space in your suitcase to take home a real Channel Island jersey or Guernsey.
- Pocket binoculars and perhaps a field guide to birds or wildflowers, if you are a keen nature buff.
- National Trust card if you have one – both Jersey and Guernsey have affiliated NT branches which allow UK members free access to their properties.

- Bucket and spade – for sandcastle architects of all ages – and snorkelling kit if you have one.
- For local holiday reading, you may be interested in Jenny Wood's account of life on Herm as the Tenant's wife, or the enthusiastic books about Jersey written by John Nettles on the making of the 1980s *Bergerac* TV series. Classics include Compton Mackenzie's novel *Fairy Gold*, based on Jethou, and Victor Hugo's *Toilers of the Sea*, set in Guernsey.

CHECK-IN & CUSTOMS

First-time travellers can often find airport security intimidating, but it is all very easy, really. If you are travelling from a large airport, check which terminal before you leave home.

- Check-in desks usually open two hours before the flight is due to depart. Arrive early for the best choice of seats.
- Look for your flight number on the TV monitors in the check-in area, and find the relevant check-in desk. Your tickets will be checked and your luggage labelled. Take your boarding card and go to the departure gate, where your boarding pass will be checked. There are no passport controls for flights to the Channel Islands, but you will go through a security check, during which your hand luggage will be X-rayed.
- In the departure area, you can shop and relax, but watch the monitors that tell you when your flight is ready to board – usually about 30 minutes before take-off. Go to the departure gate shown on the monitor and follow the instructions given to you by airline staff.

CUSTOMS' ALLOWANCES

The Channel Islands are not full members of the European Union, and allowances are less generous than between other member states. At the time of writing, you may take only 200 cigarettes, a litre of spirits, 60ml perfume or £145 worth of other goods including gifts and souvenirs either into the Channel Islands or back to the UK. Check with your travel agent or tour operator for up-to-date information.

During your stay

BEACHES

Jersey is surrounded by some of the swiftest currents and highest tides in the world. West coast beaches are exposed to powerful Atlantic breakers – wonderful for experienced surfers, but unsuitable for weak swimmers. Never try to cross a causeway or explore sea caves without checking the tide tables and pay attention to warning signs. Do not swim if red flags are flying (see Beach Safety information on page 120). Lifeguards are stationed on some of the more popular beaches in summer. Other beaches may be safe for swimming but not have lifeguards or life-saving amenities available. If in doubt, check with your local representative or hotel.

⬤ *Some beaches have strong currents*

CHILDREN'S ACTIVITIES

Most Jersey residents will welcome children and there is plenty for them to do. There are attractions and sporting activities aimed at children, and the many fortifications scattered all over Jersey make tempting places for children to play and hide. Do remember, however, that some castles and ruins are derelict and may be dangerous to explore.

BEACH SAFETY

A flag system is used to warn bathers when sea conditions are unsafe for swimming.

- **Red flag** = dangerous conditions, no swimming
- **Yellow** = good swimmers only, apply caution
- **Green** = safe bathing conditions

TOURIST INFORMATION

Jersey's main Tourist Information Office is in the States of Jersey Tourism Office, Liberation Square, St Helier (☎ 01534 500888).

CURRENCY

Sterling is acceptable in Jersey, as it is on all the Channel Islands, so you don't need to change any money. Jersey issues its own coins and banknotes, but these are not legal tender in the UK. Travellers' cheques, UK cheques backed by a banker's card and major credit cards are all widely accepted methods of payment. There are no cash dispensers on the smaller islands.

ELECTRICITY

Jersey has the same voltage as the UK, 240 volts AC, and uses British style three-pin sockets.

GETTING AROUND

Car hire & driving A hired car is the most popular way to explore Jersey and rental rates are very reasonable. Traffic congestion is a serious problem on Jersey, which has many narrow lanes and blind bends, often

EMERGENCIES

☎ Dial 999 for police, fire, ambulance or coastal rescue services.

lined with unforgiving granite walls or ditches, and no footpaths. Great care is needed on the roads at all times. Choose the smallest car you can tolerate, because the lanes are too narrow for large vehicles. Hired cars are marked with a large letter H, but locals are surprisingly tolerant of bewildered tourists blundering round their lanes. Remember that you must have a valid driving licence with no endorsements for dangerous or drunk driving in the last five years. You must be aged 21 years and over.

Speed limits The maximum speed limit is 65 km/h (40 mph) on Jersey. In towns it is 40 km/h (25 mph) and on Green Lanes it is only 25 km/h (15 mph). If visiting Guernsey remember the maximum speed limit is 55 km/h (35 mph).

Rules of the road As in the UK, you drive on the left. A yellow line across a minor road means STOP. You must give way to traffic on the major road. Yellow arrows painted on the road warn of an approaching stop line, while a single yellow line along the side of the road means no parking at any time. A yellow box painted at a junction indicates a 'filter in turn' system. This simply means that all approach roads have equal priority, so you take it in turns with cars from other directions. Remember drink-driving penalties are strict.

Roads In general the road surfaces are good and road markings clear, but be aware that some roads are extremely narrow and have ditches either side – these are known as Green Lanes. They may have granite walls either side that can leave a nasty dent in the side of your car if driving recklessly – a good reason not to exceed the 25 km/h (15 mph) limit.

Petrol Petrol is cheap and a tankful goes far. Don't buy more than £5 worth at a time – most firms expect you to take the car back empty.

Parking Parking regulations are very strictly enforced, even with visitors. In St Helier and one or two other popular places, parking is by a paycard system. Paycards are available from shops, post offices and garages displaying the symbol, or from Jersey Tourism. You are required to scratch off the appropriate time and date as instructed and leave it visible in your car. Other areas use parking discs, obtainable from St Helier Town Hall. A paycard or disc is not required from 17.00 to 08.00 or on a Sunday. There is free parking for disabled 'Orange Badge' holders.

Public transport Jersey has the second highest proportion of motor vehicles per head of population in the world behind Guernsey. Needless to say, there are jams in the busier parts of the island, but it's surprising how quickly traffic disperses on all those tiny lanes. If you don't care to drive, buses operate along the main roads, and you can always hire a bike. Jersey also has a splendid network of 'Green Lane' footpaths and coastal trails which take you through gorgeous scenery away from the cars and madding crowds. The tourist offices produce excellent, clear walks leaflets which avoid busy roads as far as possible. The cliff path on the north coast of Jersey takes you past the best of the islands' scenery.

Bus Jersey has a good bus system, though services are less frequent off season, in the evenings, and on Sundays. An Explorer ticket will allow you to hop on and off as much as you like. Most services radiate from St Helier bus station (☎ 01534 877772 for information and timetables). There are frequent services from the main towns to the airports.

Taxis Taxi ranks can be found in St Helier and at the airport. Be aware that there are different tariffs applied for day and night hire and on public holidays. Extra charges may be charged for waiting time.

Ferries Travel between Jersey and mainline UK, France and the islands of Guernsey, Alderney, Sark and Herm is easy from St Helier. Try Condor Ferries (☎ 0845 345 2000 ⓦ www.condorferries.com).

HEALTH MATTERS

All doctors, dentists and opticians operate private practices on Jersey but British visitors enjoy free medical treatment while they are on the islands. Not all costs are covered, and you are strongly advised to take out health insurance. Urgent dental problems, such as a sudden abscess, may be treated as medical emergencies. There is no need to take any forms with you, such as an EHIC medical card (which replaced the E111) but you do need to provide photographic proof of identity and UK citizenship to obtain treatment (for example a driving licence). Prescription charges are much lower than in the UK, but do take with you any medicines you need on a regular basis.

Health hazards Note that, with around 2,000 hours of sunshine a year, it is easy to get sunburned on Jersey. Despite a sea breeze, the air is clear and the ultra-violet is strong so you will need high factor sun protection.

Clinics The General Hospital in Gloucester Street, St Helier runs a free morning clinic ☎ 01534 725241 ⏰ Open Mar–Sept Mon–Sat; Oct–Feb Mon, Wed and Fri only

PERSONAL COMFORT & SECURITY

Crime prevention Happily, crime (especially personal violence or street theft) is rare in Jersey. Even so, there are a few precautionary measures to take: for example, even if the islanders themselves don't always lock their doors, it makes sense for visitors to do so. Don't leave temptation in anyone's way and you are unlikely to suffer any losses. Take care of your personal property as you would at home.

Lost property Report any loss or theft to your holiday representative or hotel staff. Notify your bank or credit card company if you lose your cheque book or credit cards. If an insurance claim is to be made you must report a theft within 24 hours to the police. The lost property office in Jersey (☎ 01534 612305) may be able to help you.

POST OFFICES

The main post office is in Broad Street, St Helier, with a network of sub-post offices dotted around the island. Jersey mail must carry Jersey stamps, and you must use the correct stamps on any post mailed from Jersey. Pillar boxes are red. The central post offices and museums in Jersey have interesting displays of local stamps, which illustrate many aspects of island life and history.

PUBLIC TOILETS
Few destinations can match Jersey for their generous provision of free, clean, unvandalized public conveniences, many suitable for visitors with disabilities.

TELEPHONES

Jersey's telecom service is modern, efficient and relatively inexpensive. Public call boxes (mostly yellow) are widespread, and use the same dialling codes as the UK. Most require cardphones, available from newsagents and post offices.

TIME DIFFERENCES

There is no time difference between Jersey and the UK, which uses Greenwich Mean Time (GMT). The clocks go forward in April and back in October.

WEIGHTS & MEASUREMENTS

Jersey operates the same metric system as in the UK.

TELEPHONING JERSEY
Jersey's dialling code from the UK is 01534.

INDEX

ACKNOWLEDGEMENTS

We would like to thank all the photographers, picture libraries and organisations for the loan of the photographs reproduced in this book, to whom copyright in the photograph belongs:
Fiona Adams (page 18); J A Brooks (page 68); J Allan Cash (pages 10, 44, 92); De Wildenberg (page 75); Guernsey Tourist Board (pages 58, 71, 76, 82, 87); Lindsay Hunt (pages 36, 48); Image Select (page 38); Jersey Tourism (pages 5, 9, 15, 17, 19, 22, 27, 34, 35, 39, 41, 43, 46, 49, 57, 53, 97, 99, 100, 102, 105, 109, 111, 119); Jupiter Images Corporation (pages 113, 125); Spectrum (pages 1, 28); Sunworld (page 107); Thomas Cook Tour Operations Ltd (pages 51, 91); VisitGuernsey (pages 83, 85, 89, 95); Eric Young (page 31).

We would also like to thank the following for their contribution to this series:
John Woodcock (map and symbols artwork);
Katie Greenwood (picture research);
Patricia Baker, Rachel Carter, Judith Chamberlain-Webber, Nicky Falkof, Nicky Gyopari, Stephanie Horner, Robin Pridy (editorial support);
Christine Engert, Suzie Johanson, Richard Lloyd, Richard Peters, Alistair Plumb, Jane Prior, Barbara Theisen, Ginny Zeal, Barbara Zuñiga (design support).

Send your thoughts to
books@thomascook.com

- Found a beach bar, peaceful stretch of sand or must-see sight that we don't feature?
- Like to tip us off about any information that needs a little updating?
- Want to tell us what you love about this handy, little guidebook and more importantly how we can make it even handier?

Then here's your chance to tell all! Send us ideas, discoveries and recommendations today and then look out for your valuable input in the next edition of this title. And, as an extra 'thank you' from Thomas Cook Publishing, you'll be automatically entered into our exciting monthly prize draw.

Send an email to the above address or write to:
HotSpots Project Editor, Thomas Cook Publishing, PO Box 227, Unit 15/16, Coningsby Road, Peterborough PE3 8SB, UK.